The Transition from Wuotanism to Christianity

Guido von List

Translated, Edited and Introduced by
Stephen E. Flowers

Copyright © 2022
Lodestar

All rights reserved. No part of this book, either in part or in whole may be reproduced, transmitted or utilized in any form or by any other means electronic, photographic or mechanical, including photocopying, recording, or by any information storage and retrieval system, without the permission in writing from the Publisher, except for brief quotations embodied in literary, scientific articles and reviews.

For permissions wrote the Publisher at the address below:

Published by:
Lodestar

seekthemysteries.com

Acknowledgements

Special thanks go to Michael Moynihan, Annabel Lee, Larry Camp and Bert Rogge, one-time President of the Guido von List Society, for the generous donation of his vintage Guido von List library to me.

Abbreviations

Fr.	French
G.	German
Lat.	Latin
NHG	New High German, Modern German

Translator's Introduction

The works of Guido von List can be divided into several categories. He wrote poetry, short stories, novels, dramas and descriptions of landscapes in addition to his expository works on myth, legend and ancient esoteric traditions. The Armanic (esoteric) works for which he is best known today can also be divided into major categories. One category of his work, which might be called analytical, is highly dependent on the German language to be fully intelligible. These are works on Germanic tribal names, primeval language and heraldry, for example. Another group is formed by works that frequently make use of his idiosyncratic linguistic theories, but are not primarily based on these practices. These works, such as *Das Geheimnis der Runen*, *Die Religion der Ario-Germanen*, *Die Armanenschaft der Ario-Germanen* and this piece, *Die Übergang vom Wuotanismus zum Christentum* are far more suitable for translation into the English language.

The general topic of this book is one that many people find very fascinating: the way in which Christianity absorbed pagan ideas and carried them forward in the guise of Christianity. List had a highly-developed attitude toward this process. He was not as pagan as some people would like him to have been, but his own "defense" is that Christianity itself was largely "paganized" in that it merely carried forth the eternal ideas of the one true and only "religion," *Armanentum*— the esoteric or secret doctrine of the initiates. So, List, just as his ancestors had done, merely understood the Christian symbolism in terms of the indigenous traditions of his own people. As it turns out, List was not as "anti-Christian" as many today would have him be. This is simply because he saw in the Christian imagery just another expression of the inextinguishable permanence of the Armanic way. It is in this book more than any other that List makes this general point most extensively.

Over the past century and a half many important scholarly studies have been devoted to the topic of the "Christianization" of the Germanic tribes. If one were to read only one of these, I would recommend James Russell's *The Germanization of Early Medieval Christianity* (Oxford, 1994). There Russell makes the reasonable point that any and all peoples subjected to coerced and widespread "conversion" from their own native or indigenous cultural values to ones from the outside and ones often at odds with their deep-seated values, will in various ways "resist" this process and will in fact re-interpret the new symbols in terms of their old and familiar ones. Today most people are familiar with the "creole" (i.e. syncretic) religious found in the Caribbean which mix Christian symbols with African and indigenous American elements. This process is by no means unique to the Caribbean, but rather is the normal and expected mode of cross-cultural interaction everywhere and throughout history. The same processes active in Haiti in recent centuries were the same as the ones made felt in Europe a thousand years ago.

In conjunction with the work of Russell, one should also become familiar with the works of G. Ronald Murphy.

One essential Listian concept comes forth in the course of this book is that what he called *Armanentum*, or the *Armanenschaft*, was and is an *esoteric* tradition which lies at the root of many, but not all "religions." It appears that to some extent List identified Armanendom with the "secret doctrine" as promulgated by the Theosophical Society by which List was greatly influenced. List believes that there was an original universal religion which he designates with the term *Wihinei* which is identical with what he also calls the *Armanenschaft*. It is purely esoteric and philosophically abstract. As misunderstanding arises in humanity, what he calls "religious systems" or "religion-systems" are developed in which mythic symbols are employed. Wuotanism is the religion-system indigenous to the Germanic folk. Such religion-systems can help people return ot the level of understanding of *Wihinei* (as Wuotanism does) or they can lead people further astray. This philosophy underlies the whole text of this book.

One thing that List strongly emphasizes in his view of the historical development of Armanism, its origin and its decline following the coming of Christianity to Germania is that the tradition had, prior to his arrival and his decoding of the secrets of the runes and the mysteries of the primeval symbolic language of the Armanen, is that his discoveries have opened the door to the conscious redevelopment of these mysteries in a renewed way. This is what he referred to as the German Rebirth— *das Deutsche Wiedergeburt*.

Guido von List, of course, approached this whole topic from his own perspective. I would like to point out that only recently a major biography of Guido von List by Eckehard Lenthe entitled *Wotan's Awakening* has been published by Dominion Press. That book should be read in conjunction with any writings by "der Meister." Lenthe does not give a particularly "objective" viewpoint about the work of Guido von List, as his attitude is more that of the *true believer*, and is valuable for that reason. A more scholarly view is offered in the introductory material to *The Secret of the Runes* (Destiny, 1988).

In the present work, List expresses many of the underlying ideas about ethnicity, culture and history that were prevalent in the German-speaking world of the late 19th and early 20th century. As one deeply steeped in the study of German history and culture, these are clear and obvious to me. However, these concepts can appear to be extremely esoteric on the surface in the 21st century. The first several pages of this book are devoted to an explanation of the esoteric cultural history of "Germany," which List understands as a Pan-Germanic realm. In his discussion of the Ing-fo-onen, the Ist-fo-onen the Armanen [or Semanen], he foreshadows the theories of Georges Dumézil.

Ultimately, many of List's ideas are most completely understood in light of the cultural and political problems of his native Austria during his own life-time, which coincidentally spans almost perfectly between the year of widespread revolutionary uprising in Europe (1848) and the end of the

Great War (WWI), 1918. List was born in 1948 and died in 1919, just seven months after the end of World War I.

This work, like the rest of List's published work, speaks directly to the question of how Guido von List's "magic" worked. List was not a ceremonial magician, although he did sometimes stage ceremonies which operated on a magical level. Writers who were directly influenced by him, e.g. Friedrich Bernhard Marby, Siegfried Adolf Kummer and E. Tristan Kurtzahn did engage in such practices influenced by his theories. List practiced what could be called "Raja Yoga" — an intellectual and analytical approach to the mysteries leading to levels of knowledge based on mystical insight.

The text of this work poses the usual challenges faced by anyone attempting to translate the idiosyncratic style and usages of the German language used by List. In recent times, some have attempted to "translate" List's works by means of a computer-generated translating program. Sometimes the results are mixed, to say the least. Frequently, because many of List's points are made by indicating the sound-qualities of his "mystery language" and Modern German words or words in other languages, I have had to resort to including the original word in square brackets with an indication of the language of the original word.

The ideology of Guido von List still requires a vast amount of unbiased scholarly investigation. Unfortunately, the academic study of the works of Guido von List has up to now been marked by extreme bias. I have sometimes been accused, especially by establishment scholars working in Western academia, of having a sympathetic or "indefensibly non-judgmental" attitude toward subjects of the Germanic renaissance of early twentieth century Germany. Of course, I could say a good deal about the ideological and financial pressures these people are obviously under to write such things. I expand on these ideas further in my book *The Revival of the Runes* (Inner Traditions, 2021). At the same time, I have been even more often chided by the "true believers" among those who identify as the *Armanen* of today who revere List unconditionally and believe that every word he wrote constitutes a sort of gospel. Both of these camps often do not much appreciate my approach. My method is best described as "sympathetic objectivity." My aim is first to convey to the reader the *actual* ideas and systems promulgated by the early twentieth century German thinkers, second, in my commentaries or notes I occasionally attempt to inform the reader where there are errors of fact in what List says. In the analysis, I will also point out what I think is motivating List (or other related writers) based on a deep knowledge of the culture and historical context from which they sprang. This hermeneutic approach to the texts is often not much valued in this early twenty-first century world, divided as it is between two highly uncritical ideological camps. In my defense, should I be thought to need one, I hope that *most* readers will appreciate my respect for them as students, and that from what I offer they can make up their own minds about things in a way that is meaningful for them individually. I am also writing material that I hope will still be respected in the far future. Many write for the present, I try to write — and even translate — from beyond the limits of the mundane.

Stephen E. Flowers
Woodharrow
June 21, 2021

The Transition from Wuotanism to Christianity

As is implicitly apparent in the discussion contained in my last work in the context of the "Germanic Rebirth" which was entitled *The Religion of the Aryo-Germanic Folk: Esoteric and Exoteric*, the religion — better expressed as the *Wihinei* — of the Aryo-Germanic folk underwent various transformations such that the "transition from Wuotanism to Christianity" in no way represents the first reorganization of the outer forms of Armanism whereby the inner kernel of Armanic teachings endured so much conceptual obfuscation. Already in much earlier pre-Christian times various other, foreign religion-systems gained influence on Wuotanism, such as for example the different cults of druidism, such as those of the Italian and Greek peoples, and especially the Romans, but regardless of such influences the cult of the individual Aryo-Germanic lands was certainly not in and of itself shaped in any uniform way. In this regard, cultic practice in fact often alternated between veneration of Wuotan (Odin) and Donar (Thor) as the main deity, so that there was even a noticeable kind of division among many folk-groups such that Wuotan, as the god of the nobles, had a special cult beside that of Donar, who was seen as the god of farmers, such that the common people themselves knew very little about Wuotan. But since such things were merely variations in the outer appearance of the divine services, peculiar features of this kind were not very important. Phenomena of this type can even be observed today in the many special customs found in certain cultic practices at places of pilgrimage that often conspicuously diverge from the general cultic practices of the Church. The opportunity to discuss the causes of such phenomena will frequently be offered during the course of the present work.

The secret doctrine of Armanism that was insinuated into the "High Secret Institution" [*Hohe Heimliche Acht*] by the

Armanen actually remained untouched by such variations and also remained so during the great process of transformation toward Christianity, but it was and is — since the great mass of the people is not able to understand this knowledge — the actual secret doctrine and as such the lodestar for the leaders of the folk, the Armanen (or Semanen[1]), and even among these only for a few of the elite.

It was previously emphasized in my work about the religion of the Aryo-Germanic folk that Armanism itself had to undergo a demise after it had reached its zenith— all according to the law of arising, becoming, transformation and passing away toward a new arising in order to rejuvenate itself that it could shine forth anew after its transitional darkening (allegorically, its winter-sleep) in a more beautiful, brighter light. Likewise it, just as every other form of phenomena in life and evolution of the cosmos, is bound to garmic[2] law, it too already bore within itself the seed of its death in its original germination, as well as the rejuvenating primeval seed of future arising, becoming, etc.

This immutable law of nature, which following the equally immutable law of homogeneity [*Gleichartigkeit*], is confirmed in every phenomenon of life, was to be — recognized? — by exact science: No! — only rediscovered and, of course, renamed. *Sapienti sat*.[3] This characteristic fact is important enough to be verified by an example:

Whenever we roam through the woods during the fall, when we see the fantastic rush of colors provided by the wild grapes, the oak leaves, the rose bushes, of the incomparable play of light in the autumnal forest, we feel a serene, clear perception of death reverberating in us, one which invokes our solitude in the world, or at least as much as our modern, educated thought processes will allow. But the majority of people silently and apathetically ignores this old familiar "common phenomena in nature"— just like all other similar occurrences. Conversely, we ask ourselves: Why then all of this glory, this beauty!? — The well-known Frankfurt botanist, Prof. Martin Moebius, maintains this chromatic splendor of autumn is only intelligible in connection with the aesthetic impulse by means of the assumption of a great general principle of nature independent of all laws of life such as those of physics, chemistry or astronomy. For, as Moebius says, "the sublime symmetry of so many leaf-formations with their systems of veins, the beauty of so many flowers as well as many rare formations on the wings of butterflies and petals of flowers, on shells as well as the feathers of birds are all at odds with every Darwinian idea of adaptation in nature, but it is to be understood with an assumption of an unconscious impulse in nature toward that which we humans call *beauty* with the hypothesis that within the impetus toward formation in nature an unknown Something is at work about which we can only say that it is probably the same thing that reveals itself in humans as the *artistic* impulse.

We are sincerely thankful to the warm-hearted botanist Professor M. Moebius for this insight, for soon the ancient Armanic knowledge will be revealed with perfect clarity that in nature there exists a fully conscious directive and not only merely an unconscious impulse toward beauty, [as well as toward happiness], which can be clearly and regularly recognized in all facets of life, as well as in the "aesthetic impulses in humanity." And modern science has clearly proven this in the field of organic chemistry, although it still provisionally shrinks from drawing the absolutely necessary conclusion on this concerning a perfectly clear conscious, all-unified, life and governance of nature according to the primal law of arising, becoming, transformation, passing away toward a new arising of individual entities, and therefore affirming the ancient secret doctrine of Armanism. Organic chemistry has actually recognized that two chemical constituents exist which counteract one another and which cause the leaf to appear green during its becoming phase, but then red in its transformative phase, and which have long been known by the names chlorophyll and anthocyanin. Chlorophyll is the agent of the most important life-functions of most plants and is both chemically and biologically in many respects is comparable to hemoglobin, the most important continuant part of red blood corpuscles in animals.

By means of its fluorescence chlorophyll has the characteristic of altering sunlight such that its entire energy benefits the increase of organic connections of the plant, converting it from inorganic matter. It is no longer formed as soon as the leaves are ready to fall and its activity ceases. But in its place anthocyanin now forms everywhere where the leaf needs protection from the incidental rays of light, for at this time that characteristic retrograde motion — or transformation — begins. All the organic compounds that have been stored in the leaves, and which the plant still needs, migrate throughout the cells and vessels far down, all the way into the hibernating trunk and into the roots. On their journey, that is reminiscent of the circulation of blood corpuscles in animals, they are however subject to the rays of the sun that would decompose and destroy them if the anthocyanin did not spread its protective red covering over them during this process. This anthocyanin has the purpose of transforming light into warmth, one type of energy into another. Therefore, it provides warmth and shade to the substance as it flows back into the trunk. The red pigment of the leaves, the anthocyanin, is therefore intended to protect the plant against the overly harsh sunlight, against being dried out as well as against freezing. So chlorophyll appears in the life of plants as the executor of the will towards arising and becoming, just as anthocyanin holds good as the executor of the will toward transformation and passing away toward a new arising, exactly as we see in the life of the cosmos: light and dark, warmth and cold, summer and winter, day and night.

And just as the exact sciences confirm here in this one example, which could be verified by many other examples, it occurs in exactly the same way with regard to the arising, becoming, transforming and passing away toward a new arising of each and every phenomenon of humanity's spiritual efforts and therefore no less with that institution we call religion. Religion too has its periodic phases corresponding to the basic law of arising, becoming, transforming and passing away toward a new arising, religion too has periods of highs and lows, but it as well is never extinguished, but rather propagates itself through the periods of the deepest decay as a "secret doctrine" in order to save the seed for a new blossoming in the next period of evolution. And this is well-established: While the secret doctrine — as the disembodied soul — is to a certain extent founded upon the primeval condition [*Urstand*]; the material direction dominates in spiritual life — as the dis-ensouled body within humanity, this is the division between faith and knowledge, because the soul has left the body; and the dis-ensouled body — knowledge without faith — now sets out upon a search for the departed soul. As soon as this "faithless knowledge" discovers the first threads of connection which lead back to the secret doctrine it is powerfully struck by fear and shortsightedly attempts to claim these advances (which are actually ancient traditions) by providing new names for the newly discovered truths while becoming suspicious of the secret doctrine as belonging to superstition.[4] But step by step modern exact science draws closer to primeval knowledge and traditions of the secret doctrine and with almost mathematical precision it will be able to calculate the date upon which exact science will have to give up its posture of rejection with regard to the secret doctrine of Armanism and comprehensively validate these things. At this moment, the gulf between faith and knowledge will be eliminated, at which moment the hour of the birth of a renewed religion will dawn, which will then come more to believe what it knows, and therefore by the same token will activate this elevated faith-knowledge in our lives.

One should not, however, believe that the present-day function of "faithless science," which they call "exact science," would therefore be a failed and useless thing, as overly enthusiastic followers of the counter current in waiting would have it; no, absolutely not! **It is the intention of the conscious guidance of the All that during the time when religion is being eclipsed, the equally eclipsed and hidden doctrines and knowledge of Armanism is being made openly available, because these same things are being provided in the service of humanity, which to a certain extent indicates a kind of preparatory, apparent** materialization for these idealized concepts, although it is not this in reality. For as long as these practically utilized new discoveries of ancient truths merely stand in the service of an as yet still completely materialistic exploitation, they will also only function imperfectly — and their forces will only fully and completely develop when the balance between the spiritual and physical is once more restored, which will only be fulfilled upon the dawning epoch of the revival of religion, with the epoch of the union of faith and knowledge. The exact sciences help to prepare for this dawning and therefore they deserve all of their worldly recognition, even if they are entirely unaware of the nature of the interests they are serving and toward which actual goals they are progressing, for this is the exact polar opposite of the one they erroneously think they are moving toward. It is also a law in the pointed directive of the All— the conscious spiritual directorate — that all currents, even those that seem to run counter-wise only contribute further to the singular goal desired by this conscious spiritual directorate. Man goes astray as long as he strives, i.e. as long as he subscribes to his own individual will with presumed disregard for the All-knowledge, for he must, whether he wants to or does not want to, nevertheless work within the intentions, and toward the goal, of the will of the All.

And the same phenomena are also made manifest in art and literature during the time period of irreligiosity and of dominant atheism. Art — whether it is painting, sculpture, architecture, theater, poetry or whatever other art form there might be — is even seen to be in decline, because it has lost it divine inner substance and with this its ideals and it has become purely materialistic — trade goods. With the fading of the old ideas, the fading of the divine inner substance, virtuosity — or the promotion of purely technical refinements — came to the forefront, things such as the constant craze for innovation, the search for a new style. Over the last sixty years our artists have used up all of the types of style employed in ancient art, and now have happily found their way to the style of the Maoris of New Zealand. But it is all merely imitation of form remaining without spiritual sympathy, and all the sweat was in no way devoted to an honest search for a real — spiritual, divine — in a revival of art having lost its soul, rather it was merely a matter of business, a marketing craze, in order to cause talk about itself because of its novel peculiarity — to emphasize its own delightful substance — for divine individuality is not part of this! — it is only a matter of not coming up short when the awards are handed out. The types of these great innovators of the art-business — the secessionists, moderns, the most modern, super-modern, the young, youngest, super-young, newest most modern, etc., etc., etc., are, however, just like the representatives of the exact sciences and in spite of everything are still in the truest sense of the phrase "seekers after God," for they feel the desolation of their condition all too acutely, they know this, and preserve it as their trade secret that they secretly whisper to one another in "sublime moments," that they "with the whole hullaballoo are making fun of God and the world, for Man just wants to live well — so long live the praiseworthy art-business"! And in spite of all this they are still "seekers after God"! At the moment when the chasm between faith and knowledge disappears, at that very same moment the gap between believing and ability will also close, and a renewed art, and with it a new style, will be born, a style which will not be based on imitation, but rather on physio-spiritual creativity. Then the creations of the superseded soulless activity will appear to have just been a confused dream and in those places where it will be preserved will constitute an obscure corner in the junk-gallery of cultural history, which we as fittingly as possible call a museum. The few artists who are transmitting these ancient ideas into the dawning age of the resurrection of the arts today certainly lead lives of martyrs, full of rejection, but they will be reborn as the masters of the renewed arts, for "the last will be first," as it is written in the Law of Garma. To them an Armanic "Alaf sal fena!"

Thus, in the same regard, the circumstances surrounding other social features seen from a purely materialistic perspective come to a crisis point in such epochs of irreligiosity ad atheism, as, just to point out a few of them: the women's question, the socialistic and anarchistic currents and so much else; but all of these currents, even if they do convulse the social and cultural order and bring it into flux, are really merely the birth pangs of the coming epoch, in the convulsions of which those chasms will be closed once more, chasms which were manifest between faith and science as well as faith and ability and this will then usher in an age in which the biune-bifidic dyadic unity: God : World, spirit : body, faith : knowledge and belief : ability will begin to arise in a new phase of arising and becoming.

Also, all of these efforts that today proceed only from purely materialistic assumptions and are guided by not entirely innocent, self-serving motives in favor of the instigators, nevertheless prepare the way, despite their contrary intentions of the conscious direction of the All — unintentionally and unconsciously — during the age of the occultation of religion laying the groundwork for the new dawning day and its blessings.

This coming day will likely be similar to the day immediately preceding the now fading night, but it will not be the same, for in the context of regular transformations an exact repetition of what has already died off never occurs, just as an entity [personality] which today is masking an individuality and which corresponds to its essence, never does so, the essence will reveal this individuality [Ichheit] upon its final incarnation just before its final death. Just as the individuality remains unaltered throughout the entire duration of creation, the respective personality is transformed upon each renewed re-incarnation and in exactly the same way each new age alters its external form, which the special character of the time provides to it by means of which it markedly distinguishes itself from its predecessors as well as its successors.

If up to now there has only been talk of "the religion" and never of "the religions," this has been done consciously, for there is only one religion, the *Wihinei*, that is, the "secret doctrine of Armanism," which is the origin of all other religions that ever existed, do now exist or that ever will exist in the future, therefore all of these "religions" are nothing other than merely "systems of religion." Such systems of religion, falsely called religions, have always been established by contemporaries for contemporaries, by people of the same kind for people of the same kind [*Artgenossen*], as they correspond to the requirements of the age and kind of people, and never had the aim — according to the intention of the founders involved — of forming a common world-religion, which in any case could only exist in the esoteric sense, but never in an exoteric arrangement of details. Since an esoteric world-religion will only become possible and necessary in a still far distant future cycle of ages, and for a long time into the future exoteric religion-systems will still remain indispensable, because — with the exception of isolated individuals within a folk-group —different peoples are still on very different levels and abilities of thinking and conceptualization, which the exoteric religion-systems have to accommodate, so therefore today, and for a long time to come, the exoteric religion-systems are necessarily arranged in different types of evolutionary levels in order gradually to attain an ever more perfect, and finally the highest, developmental level, which is precisely that esoteric religion, or better-said— the esoteric *Wihinei* itself. In this gradual rise of exoteric religion-systems they are developed to the level of the esoteric *Wihinei*, which is actually as ancient as humanity itself, but it is only possessed by a few especially favored ones the secret doctrine of Armanism, which comes into effect — as has been repeatedly pointed out — most certainly again through the law of arising, becoming transforming, passing away to a new arising and actually in the form of a cycle of time in a spiral shape [like a snail-shell] to attain the next level or epoch. Accordingly, each epoch (circle of time, cycle, ring, etc.) possesses its own particular exoteric religion-system that simultaneously has marked with this cycle of time its arising (its founding), its becoming (its zenith), its transformation (its fixation of form, dogmas) and finally its passing away to a new arising (its extinguishment, time of irreligiosity, atheism). The history of religions and cultures offers thousands of examples of this as evidence of observation and as proof. But since these cycles of time to a great extent influence one another an extremely complex web-work arises, that, upon initial superficial glance, may appear to be confused and irregular, but to the sober and knowledgeable observer it is easily broken down into its individual magical currents and the divinely artistic meshing of these transports the observer to amazed admiration.

Following these necessary introductory observations on the laws of development and decay in which the rigorous laws in all events in the life of the All as well as of every individual being can clearly be seen, we will now enter into the description and interpretation of the actual processes which introduce and complete the transition from Wuotanism to Christianity.

In the storms of the more than five-hundred-year long struggle of the Aryo-Germanic powers with Roman knavery, i.e. during the time between fifteen years before the beginning of our era and the year 488 after the beginning of that age, the Aryo-Germanic worldview, as well as its religious system called "Wuotanism," suffered its most awful convulsion, and its most dangerous injury. Apparently, the power of the previous world-view proved itself to be no longer suited to contemporary conditions, for during the destructive whirlwinds of this epoch the glittering Roman arts of seduction and deception overcame the mind-set of the Germans, which was cultivated by the Armanen, and directed toward loyalty and truth, the folk slowly lost its trust in its gods and so in themselves as well. This trust was increasingly shattered as the folk became aware of how, in the beginning sporadically, but later increasingly often, their princes, initially out of necessity and the drive for self-preservation, but then out of conceit, selfishness and in the end out of base greed, forgot their duties, broke their contracts and oaths, and finally often in unconscious but often even in conscious faithlessness they go astray against the folk, tribe and even against their own families, and the momentary seeming outer success deceived them and their folk through the conjured up inestimable damages that threw them and their folk into garmic chains[5] centuries and centuries ago. The princes were, however, themselves Armanen, ones of knowledge, and so their example had an especially disenchanting and destructive effect on the folk itself. Then it occurred that one of the most important institutions of the ancient Aryo-Germanic *Rita*[6] was gravely shattered and in the course of this half millennium almost entirely forgotten. One of the three branches of Yggdrasil began to wither, as one skald [Arman] said.

Going back to the primeval age, the Aryo-Germanic folk was divided into three estates — the three branches of Yggdrasil — and these are the Ing-fo-onen, the Armanen [or Semanen] and the Ist-fo-onen.[7] The Ing-fo-onen were the settled families and their elders [according to today's standards the owners of inherited estates] who managed the family possessions. All members of the folk had to belong to the Ing-fo-onen class, not excepting the king, for the Ing-fo-onen formed the producer-class. The Armanen, or Semanen, were the men of knowledge, the learned, priests and judges in one person. They had to be Ing-fo-onen and were not allowed to leave this estate or class. Since all princes and kings were Armanen, the class of Armanen is the cradle of the original aristocracy as well as the cradle of the high nobility. Initially Armanendom, and with it nobility, was only connected to a singular entity [person] and only later became inheritable. They formed the teaching class. The Ist-fo-sonen were the excess population who had to emigrate when the family possessions or the "Alemende," the possessions of the folk, that is, the land, was no longer able to feed them. According to Rita they marched out in orderly fashion under the leadership of an army-leader (G. *Herzog*) and a few counts (G. *Grafen*) at the time of the Ostara-festival, intent upon obtaining land after they had sacrificed their old name [*ver sacrum*](a) and received a new one in its place under which they entered history as a new folk-group. They founded new realms as colonies and only when they had made themselves independent of their original tribal land did the war-leader take on the title of king. They formed the class of migrants. The enormous expenditure of human beings caused by the half-millennium of Roman wars, however, transformed the migratory class into a warrior class as we understand our military class today. The Ist-fo-sonen became Rahakater,[8] that is, vengeance fighters, out of which later developed the famous "heroes" of saga and song, and later still the mercenaries, until they eventually in the end turned into the *Kreisläufer* at the end of the eighteenth century. Through this reformation of the migratory class into the warrior class the planned colonial aims, according to *Rita*, of reserve and trained excess population was squandered with regard to any war-aims, for soon the Ist-fo-onen also formed standing troops of soldiers in the Roman army, as the Gentes Alemanorum, Gentes Marcomanorum, Gentes Quadorum, etc., in the service of foreign powers (similar to the foreign legions of today), but since, through the many centuries, this excess population soon acquired more of a taste for free-reign soldier-life than for the serious work of restrained colony-building which was to the detriment of Aryo-Germanic folk-vitality, and this promoted cultural fertilization of foreign nations hostile to Germanic values. For, as the migrations ceased, they again turned to emigration, but in the meantime the *Rita* had been forgotten, and without forming colonies at present hundreds of thousands emigrate from Aryo-Germanic countries annually to America, Africa and Australia. They do not form colonies but rather perish in individualistic struggles for their existence in foreign nations, strengthening these with their Aryo-Germanic blood in a common struggle against the Aryo-Germanic folk. This is the withered branch of the world-ash Yggdrasil. To make it once more verdant would be one of the most important and noble tasks of the emigrant associations and of the state generally. By far the largest part of the Aryo-Germanic colonies of the pre-Roman age were lost in this way because the fresh supply of population ceased: thus with the possessions in the Crimea, the Balkans, North Africa, even in central and northern Italy and in Spain.[9] Therefore the Roman colonies penetrated into the heart of Germania poisoning the minds and culture of the folk. No less also Slavs, Mongols and Mongoloids came out of the East which in a very similar manner, even if in a different form, damaged Germania, for: "More worms than foolish ninnies imagine lie below the ash and entwine the roots of the world-tree constantly." [Edda: Grimnismal].

It is very noteworthy that the name Aryan, which is attested as being very ancient in both language and symbolism, only occurs in many circumlocutions in isolated names of certain tribes in Germania,[10] but nowhere is it to be found as a basic element up to the fifth century of our time reckoning in the names of the peoples of Germania. This can be very simply explained in that all Aryo-Germanic peoples knew themselves to be Aryans and considered themselves as such and left the obvious unexpressed in their many specialized names which emphasized what was characteristic just as today we do not stress our belonging to a particular racial group in any kind of name, because we too leave the obvious unmentioned.

Then, in the fifth century there suddenly appeared a folk-name in which the designation "Aryan" occurred with definite intention and it was the folk-name *Ripuarians*, and virtually at the same time their other name: *Franks*. Their region was the eastern bank of the Rhine between the Frisians and Alemanni and later they extended themselves onto the western bank of the Rhine as far as the Mosel. They first appear as the *Provincia Ripuarorum* also and *Ducatum et Pagum Ripuarorum* and *Ravennas*, the geographer of the seventh century [published by Jacob Gronorius in 1698] called their region Fancia Rhinensem. Jordanes — around 450 — garbles this as Riparioli. Their laws, known as the *Salic Law*, were the basis for the *Lex Ripuarium* from the middle of the sixth century, as well as the *Capitular* of King Dagobert [628-639].

The name "Ripuarian," erroneously derived from *riva*, "river-bank," led to the view that these were to be understood as "riverbank Aryans," which is obviously an error, as folk-groups have never been designated by banks or shores, since there has never been a folk-group that was not settled on some sort of shoreline. And why should an account of such a meaningless thing, the concept of "Aryan" be emphasized in this particular name? — Of course, the reason lies deeper, for the name is clear enough: *ripa* means "to divide off," but *ripu* means "the one who has been divided off," therefore the Ripuarians are those who divided themselves off from the Aryan world [G. *Ariertum*], those who had separated themselves from Aryan law and religion, as they accepted Roman law and Roman religion— Christianity. Through several centuries as a Roman province they had already been Romanized, they had already been weaned off of the Aryan law as well as Aryan religion (Wuotanism). After the demise of the Roman Empire the desire arose in them to assume the heritage of Rome, and such desires for power and dominion prepared for the efforts which would be actualized by Karl the Great (Charlemagne), the Saxon-slaughterer (*selactenaere*). For this reason, they called themselves the "Freemen" [*Franken*], that is, those free from the Aryan *Rita*. Therefore, their Armanen suddenly appear as "Salians" [people of salvation], and therefore the "Salic Law" appeared, which although still rooted in the ancient Aryan *Rita*, still means a separation from it. So here the concept of "Aryan" was first used as a qualifier in the name "Ripuarian" and found its justification and meaning, and it is for this reason it is first found contained in this name. No event in the development of nations occurs without being prepared for, and thus it was with the catastrophe that the age of Charlemagne signified, which occurred by means of the separation of the Franks from the Aryan league and this was the condition which made it possible for the creation of France, the formation of the French language, for the demise of the Lakkobards

[Langobards], for the cruel damage done to the Germanic peoples on the Iberian, Italian and Balkan peninsulas, as well as finally the fall of Wuotanism itself with all of its tragic results.

This separation from the Aryan league also caused the divorce of the Frankish *Armanen* from that organization and their re-naming as the Salians, additionally a similar split occurred among the *Armanen* in the, for the time being, still unified other Aryo-Germanic populations.

Even those who paid homage to Rome soon formed a powerful party and the followers of the ancient *Rita* increasingly fell into a minority, and this occurred to such a degree that they were forced to form secret societies in order to take the ancient Aryan *Wihinei* into the *Hohe Heimliche Acht*. Thus originated the secret societies of the *Vehm*, the *Kalanders* and may others, the former to take the secret law and the *Rita*, the latter to take the ancient Aryan *Wihinei* up into the *Hohe Heimliche Acht*. That band of Armanen of the true old school who preserved the law called themselves the fellows, the *Vehm* or *Feme* [still today in Dutch a guild or corporation is called *veeme*, i.e. those who belong together] or the *Femanen*.[11] these preserved the ancient Aryan *Rita* especially according to this one principle: that every Aryo-German is a free man, he may not be the lord or serf of any other Aryo-German." They held the ancient, freely attended Thing-assemblies at the ancient sacred places [*Halgadomen*], the holy old Thing-steads, and when it was later no longer possible to hold these publically "under the shining sun," they did so in a concealed way at midnight at the abandoned Thing-steads or at other remote locations in the dark of the forest, strictly kept secret and marked with a red cross known to the cunning. It is for this reason that there are many red crosses found in lonely places in the woods and found in the names of fields and other locals.[22] The other division of the *Armanen*, which had dedicated itself to the care of the ancient Aryan *Wihinei*, in order to preserve this early on, for later when they could no longer resist the onslaught of the new era, they endeavored to transmit the ancient Aryo-Germanic

Wihinei into Christianity, and called themselves the *Kalanders* and their secret language and secret symbolism was called *Kala*.

Here it is absolutely necessary to discuss in more detail the literal and symbolic meaning of the concept *Kala* and all of its derivative subordinate and resulting concepts and to establish these in order to be able to explain what follows.

The *ur*-word *kal* is the basis for the concepts naked, bare [G. *kahl*], call out, scream [G. *kallen*, "chatter"] turn, twist [*kalun*, from which G. *Kalaunen*: "intestines"], source [G. *Quelle*, wedge [G. *Keil*], keel, etc. and combined with *sa*, "compose" from which skald [*sa-kal-de*], the poet; but it also means "time" in a transferred sense, as "that which turns itself" or "the changing" along with numerous other derivations and side formations.[13] In relation to the meaning of "turning" and "changing" a few small examples may expand our viewpoint. From *kalun* the concept of *Kalauer*, as a designation of "word-play by turning the meaning around," is derived; the same is true for the *Kalawn* of the Anglo-Saxons, for the English still have this word "clown," and view this as an incontestable national treasure, while the word and concept belongs to the primeval Aryo-Germanic heritage. No less does this good German conceptual word *Kaländer* belong to the word-stem *kal* in the meaning of all things having to do with *kalen*, that is, "turning," "spinning," "changing" and to this also belongs the ancient *Zeitkaländer* that looks similar to the face of a clock with a disk fitted with movable hands (out of which the clock-face was later developed) in order to indicate the "changing" of time through *Kalun* [= g], that is, the turning of the hands. Certain people interested in purifying the language like to point out that the good German word *Kaländer* (not *Kalender*] perfectly belongs to the heritage of our Aryo-Germanic German language, and has nothing to do with the Latin *calendis*, although it springs from the same root, and that they can, along with many another linguistic monstrosity, leave behind their ugly neologism *Zeitweiser* [G. "time-shower"] back where their equally overzealous predecessors of about a hundred years ago deposited neologisms such as *Riechhorn* ["smelling-horn"] because they thought the good German word *Nase* ["nose"] was supposedly derived from the Latin *naso*. Thank God that our Aryan ancestors not only already knew how to measure time for a considerable age before the Latin language even existed, but also had a calendar without having to depend on its Latin designation. A good deal more surprising things could be shown, but only one more word needs to be mentioned, and that is one reclaimed from French appropriation— the "Calembourg." As is well-known Calembourg is completely within the same category as the *Kalauer* [pun] a witty game with altered — [*verkalten*] — words. It is purely German and is simply a back-formation from *Kalenburg* or *Kalenberg*, by which no berg (high-ground) and no burg (structure) but rather a *Berge* (shelter) [concealment, hiding place] is to be understood. Therefore, the concept *Kalenberg* [*Calembourg*] signifies a **meaning concealed (*verkalt*) through the alteration of the meaning of the word**. Later we will come back to the *Kalenberge* and other *Kala*-places. As we saw above, the interpretation of the word Kaländer is such that it has to do with that which alters itself through *kalen* (turning, changing) and as a result the meaning of the word *Kaländer* is an designation for all concealed *Armanen* who, through secreting [*Verkalung*], appeared to be something different than what they actually were: Christians instead of Wuotanists or pagans.

The Calender-brotherhoods, as they were called throughout the Middle Ages, later— like all of the similar corporations derived from the *Armanen* that we will come to talk about — completely forgot their purpose and aim, so that by the fifteenth century they served as a completely Christian brotherhood and today their name is entirely misunderstood. It is erroneously assumed that the name *Kaland*, *Caland* or *Calend* comes from the idea that the clerics of a chapter or diocese met on the first Monday of each month (Lat. *calenda*). Still today in some regions of Germany this expression is used to designate regular pastoral conferences. In the Middle Ages companies of men and women, clerics and laymen, gathered under the supervision of the bishop to ensure their members a blessed burial and requiem mass for those who belonged, along with a sharing of devotions and any necessary support: Kaland-associations, *Kaland*-brotherhoods or *Kaland*-gentlemen (Lat. *Fratres Calendarii*) but their gathering was simply called a *Kaland*. The oldest one is mentioned around 1220 in the Ottberg monastery. Soon they are found throughout Germany, in Switzerland, in Hungary, France and Sweden. In the Reformation Age the *Kaland*-brotherhoods were for the most part dissolved in the Protestant countries and their often-considerable properties turned to other welfare institutions. Still at the beginning of the nineteenth century there was a *Kaland*-brotherhood in Brilon in the archdiocese of Cologne.[14] Its origins may with certainty be placed toward the beginning of the fifth century or at the earliest the middle of the fourth century, and probably close to the same time as the name *Ripu-Arian* originated and Christianity began to put down roots in Germany.

The previously mentioned intention of the Franks to aspire toward the heritage of Rome after the collapse of its position as a world-power and to spread their dominion over the rest of Germania and, if possible, over all of Europe, supported by the organization they inherited from the Romans which had been further cultivated by the Roman provincials who remained in the country and by those natives who had been influenced by them, found in the kings of the Franks the most suitable representatives and promoters. In the course of a five-hundred year Roman rulership on the left-bank of the Rhine (*Provincia Germania*) the Germanic peoples and the Romans learned to live together there in a state, interacted and mixed with one another, but certainly not everywhere to the same degree and in no way completely, but nevertheless to such an extent that the institutions and customs of life were mutually adopted, influenced or accommodated by one another. The result was that the Germanic folk — the later Franks, the Ripuarians — accepted Christianity in its Roman form while on the other hand the Romans who remained in the country transitioned into the life-style of the (Frankish) Germanic farmers and warriors. Cologne was the capital of this formational Frankish Empire, and from there the first attempts were mounted to win over the rest of Germania to Christianity. Other similar attempts were made in other parts of Germania, but with little to no success, because it was precisely there where Roman culture had not penetrated so deeply into the folk and the nationalistic feelings and ideas of these people formed a powerful resistance. Thus we observe (for example from the *Vita santi Sevreni* of the abbot Eugippius at the end of the fifth century) that in the eastern realm on the Danube in the city of Favianis (today Mautern on the Danube, Lower Austria) there lived St. Severin, who, however, in no way was — as is erroneously assumed — concerned with the spread of Christianity as its apostle, rather he limited himself to consoling and protecting the provincials in the Danube region who were left in the lurch by the Roman withdrawal. Very noteworthy and informative is the behavior of Gisa the noble queen of the Rugians in her royal fortress Stein (today a prison) near Chremisa (today Krems on the Danube), behavior which demonstrated her awareness of power with regard to the insolence of Severin, who therefore, just as Eugrippius did, spoke very ill of her and cast all sorts of suspicions and aspersions on her. And strangely, on the exact spots where we know Roman Christianity was first planted, we find *Kalands* and *Kala*-places, such as, for example, in Paris with "Our Lady" (Notre Dame) and its guardian Saint Genevieve (more about her later), the monastery of Saint Bathild, called Cala [Fr. Chelles]. In Cologne, the "old holy Cologne," there is a Kaland-brotherhood in Brilon, and near Vienna we find the Kahlenberg which at one time was called Zeizoberg (*mons conscetius*) with its ancient Kahlenbegerdorf, the Kalenderberg near Medling (Medl = "little maid"; there once existed a sanctuary [*Halgadom*] for women healers.[15] Furthermore, just to name a few more *Kala*-places, the castle Calenberg around Hannover, about which, and this is very noteworthy, the same cover story is told as for the Kahlenberg near Vienna; Kahla in the district of Roda [sic] of the Dutchy of Sachsen-Altenburg; Kalau or Calau, a market town in Lower Lusatia; Kalberg near Danzig; Kallendorf in Mähren; Kallenbrunn in Lower Austria; then in Germany: Calbe on the Milde, Calbe on the Saale; Calcar, Callies, Calvörde, Calw, Gallehuus, Geilenkirchen, Kalk, Kalanderberg near Chur, Kall, Kalle, Kalies, Kaltennordheim, Kahlgrub, -furth, -scheidt, Kolberg, Kolmar, Kolbermoor, Kolbitz and along with numerous other *Kala*-places, additionally the Kalt Kuchl (cooled Koke, i.e. cave, refuge) on the Schneeberg near Vienna. All of these place-names, however, indicate locations where Kalands existed, and the legends told about most of these locally point to a concealment [*Verkalung*] of their meanings, as they are otherwise unintelligible, and became even more unintelligible by means of the mania of connecting them to historical events or personalities, for they are, nothing other than the **preservers and protectors of mysterious truths by means of alterations of words and meanings, that is true to their names: Kalenbergs.**

A very special group of these Kalenbergs is formed by the hundreds, if not thousands, of existing "Calvary-bergs," that are usually small, isolated, often artificially built up, hills on top of which is the crucifix accompanied by the two thieves' crosses and by statues of Mary and John and which serve as the culmination of the so-called way of the cross with its "fourteen stations of the cross." These Calvary hills are imitations of Golgotha and are intended to bring Christ's work of salvation into the visible experience of local believers. In most cases with regard to this, in the case of genuinely ancient Calvary hills without exception we have in these hills old Germanic sheltering hills or tumuli [Leeberge, Hünenbetten, Hünengräber (pre-historic graves or barrows)], which were supposed to be removed from the Wuotanist cult by means of placing these Christian places of devotion on them. Up until now the name was erroneously explained as 'skull-place" (after the Lat. *calvaria* = skull) in order to hide its true meaning. This term is clearly based on *kal* (*Kala*) — transformation and *varjan* = "preserve"; therefore meaning

"Preserved in transformation"; which indicates that the old shelter-hill was preserved from destruction or desecration by — apparently! — being turned into a Christian shrine. To the cunning man the designation Calvary-hill expresses through *Kala* that which such hills would have meant *to him*. But it was a well-known *Armanic art* to conceal truths behind words with double-meanings, the decoding of which was only possible for the man of cunning— through the mystery-language, the primeval language, according to certain rules, an art that was also called *Kala*. With the original meaning of the *Kalander*, which has already been explained, there is no longer any question as to what kind of secrets the *Kala* had to conceal in order that these might be preserved for another, more fitting, time for the cunning folk to decode. The legends and legendary reports concerning the Kahlenberg near Vienna provide the desired solution, and also the key to the decipherment of all other legends concerning *Kala*-locations as far as these are known.

Sometime before the year 1337 the Zeizzoberg was already called Kahlenberg — although the time when this renaming took place cannot be documented — but it did not bear the name it does today (Leopoldsberg), there were two men named in connection with the Kahlenberg, men who count among the most mysterious people from the Middle Ages, and who have resisted all previous efforts to interpret them. Their well-known names are, however: Wigand von Theben, the pastor of the Kahlenberg and Otto Nithart Fuchs; called the peasants' enemy! The learned Sebastian Münster already names the former in this famous *Kosmographey* (Basel, 1564, page 974): "the curious parson and vicar of Calenberg about whom all of Germany knows stories," despite this, however, no one has succeeded in proving the historical reality of this personality, which, using the methods of investigation employed up to now remains impossible, as we will see. The other one, the jolly alderman Duke Otto the Merry, whose beautiful grave memorial is situated on the outside of the Cathedral of St. Stephen in Vienna, is, of course, proven to be a historically verified personality, but much of a mysterious nature is concealed behind this legendary figure such that the supposition is not unsubstantiated **that these two designations belong to one and the same personality**, and "Wigand von Theben, the pastor of Kahalenberg," was only a cover-name for Otto Nithart Fuchs, that he may have made use of on certain occasions. In order for this to become more intelligible, more information will have to be brought out.

The name "Wigand" is analyzed according to *Kala* as "sanctified or dedicated to the *other* one." The apparent place-name "Theben," which was mistakenly associated with Theben on the Danube, has, however, never been proven to be Wigand's home, and refers to Wuotanism, or actually Armanism, in a way similar to how today the concept "church" indicates "Christianity." Therefore, the name "Wigand von Theben" indicated **the one who is dedicated to the other faith, whose beliefs will be resurrected**. This is made even more clear by the additional title "pastor of the Kahlenberg," by which no Christian priest is intended, which is proven by the many pastor-hills [G. *Pfaffenberge*] that exclusively indicate Wuotanic Halgadoms and shelter-hills. Also, the concept *Pfaffe* is formed from the primal words *fa* (*pa, pfa*) and *fe*, which means "spiritually generative," and indicates the *Arman* as a priest of Wuotan, here primarily as a *Kalander*. Later, in any case, when the original meaning of the word had become obscure, the concept was transferred in a real sense to the Catholic priesthood as "castle priest" [G. *Burgpfaffe*] or "priest who says mass" [G. *Messpfaffe*], but this was, when not being done in a mocking manner, mostly only used in a less reverential way than the designation "priest." The pastor is in the true sense therefore the priest of Wuotan (heathen priest, priest of Baal, skald, bard) and here, as "pastor of Kahlenberg," to be viewed as "the **hidden caretaker of Wuotanism and the director of its passing away toward a new arising**," in which role he took care of the teachings, customs, and history of Wuotanism with ingeniously turned — *verkalten* — words and actions (funny stories) [G. *Schwänke*] according to kalic laws, he hid and thereby preserved them bequeathing them to a future generation. Certainly, all the funny stories ascribed to him today are not actually by him, and even those that are by him have been in many cases garbled, but those in the know can succeed after some meditative efforts separate the wheat from the chaff. For this reason, the seat of the (Wuotan's) pastor, the ancient Armanic Halgadom on the Zeizzo-Hill (*mons Cetius*) would be called, significantly enough, the Kahlenberg, once Wuotanism had been suppressed, since it "preserved secretly" (*verkalt barg*) that which was no longer publically acknowledged, or better said, no longer allowed to be acknowledged, but in spite of this it was secretly cared for by everyone.

All the legends of the Kahlenberg are only understandable in this context, and actually in the threefold interpretation corresponding to the kalic laws. The *first interpretation* is the one we know today according to tradition, which appears to have been calculated to deceive the opponents of Wuotanism (as do all genuine legends and folk tales) and the meaning of which follows the literal interpretation. The *second interpretation* calculated in the exoteric sense for the faithful folk in the sense of "Wuotanism as a system of religion," conceals the framework of Wuotanism behind deceptive historical entities and events. By way of example, the historical Margravine Agnes von Babenberg conceals the Asynja Idunna in the legend about her veil (the leaves on the trees), robbed from her her by storms in the autumn, but the veil is restored to her in the spring after seven months (the margravine received it back after seven years). The third interpretation in the profound esoteric understanding of the school of those in the known in the sense of "*Wihinei* or secret doctrine of the Armanen," the exalted mysteries of arising, becoming, transitioning, passing away and new-arising is concealed behind the legend of the veil. The veil of the margavine, the veil of the goddess is, to the knowledgeable, the external, perceivable part of the secret doctrine, the religion-system that comes and goes, while the internal — the *Wihinei* — that which prevails eternally remains. The veil, recovered again after seven months, or seven winters, the dark chasm between death and rebirth, is the new eternal form of an appearance of a renewed, reborn system of religion, that, according to the prophesy, is supposed to be the ancient (now rediscovered) veil, this one is, however, similar to the old one only insofar as the esoteric value manifests itself in a new appearance, which accommodates contemporary necessities.

The same exact levels of interpretation belong to the "violet festival" which is historically documented from the year 1337, thanks to its tragicomical conclusion. Otto Nithart Fuchs, the jolly councilor to Duke Otto the Merry, found the first violet of spring, covered it with his hat as a sign of his taking possession of it, and made haste to the court in order to have it acknowledged by the duke. Ancient custom required that the first violet was to be picked by a pure virgin. When the court had assembled at the place where the round-dance was supposed to begin, Otto Nithart Fuchs lifted his hat but instead of the violet he found the place a less than aromatic befouled mess. The duke, thinking that his jolly councilor had pulled an overly risky prank, grew angry, but the jolly councilor himself grew even more angry. In a rage, he ran toward the Kahlenberg village, where he found some peasants who had affixed his violet to a pole and were dancing around it in a ring. He cruelly went forth among these with a drawn sword and slayed a few of them, and for this reason he got a name of abuse: "Peasant-Enemy."

The first interpretation of this custom, according to the previous example of the legend of the veil, appears to be the solemn retrieval of the first violet of spring as a popular festival which the duke also celebrates together with his courtly state. But the peasants, for one reason or another, wanted to celebrate it separately among themselves, which caused the unwholesome outcome. This violet-festival is, however, nothing other than the spring-time festival celebrated everywhere, that is still today symbolized by the name *Märzveilchen* (sweet violet), literally "March-violet," and continues to be remembered as such, which is supposed to express joy over the new awakening of nature. The second, exoteric, interpretation for the folk who are believers in the Wuotanic sense, find in the violet a symbol of the youthful Earth-goddess, as she is being enflamed to love for the young Sun-god, and hallows the folk's own human love through this sanctifying ritual for the divine pair of lovers. The violet (G. *Feigel*) was sacred to the youthful Earth-goddess (Freya, Ostara, Giperahta, Genofeva, Gerda, etc.) and therefore it served as a salutation of the goddess who dispenses life-force to the most beautiful girl, and for the same sacred reason people danced around the first violet in a "turning," "love-awakening" ring; for through the rotation|16| |ᛋ ᛋ| in the thunderhead cloud the lightning bolt — the heavenly fire of generation | ᛋ | is created in a way similar to the turning of the yule-log (Ash) in the yule-nook (Embla) — so thus the temporal generative fire is produced, and in the mystic equation the "turning of the dance" as the magically empowered impetus toward love — the human generative fire — became for the sacred ritual of divine service in the religion of Wuotan. With this knowledge, it also becomes clear as to why the Church prohibited dancing, as well as the "flute and fiddle enticing people to dance," and exhorted them to asceticism. The third esoteric interpretation for those in the know is also present in the name, for *feigel*, as *fene*, *fane*, *faninr* (fanny), etc. which are nominal forms developed from the stem *fa* (*feigel* = *fei-ge-el* = fire gives god), with respect to the *Ur-Fyr* (primeval fire), the divine generative fire — that is, God as Creator of the All | ☉ | — Armanism recognized the sum total of the work of humanity in the constant ennobling progressive development of mankind, toward the advanced breeding of a noble race in order thereby to make humanity ever more like the gods and therefore ever more able to perfect the creation of God on Earth, along with all the rights, but with this all the duties as well. This esoteric teaching proves itself to be the true wisdom — *situlih*(b) — in that it looked out for the good of the folk and the good of the descendants through a fortunate guidance of material affairs and therefore could effectively confront all aberrations, and this overawed the decadent Romans with a sincere admiration.[17] True wisdom promoted everything that accords with the laws of nature such as in the life of the folk (cf. the Ist-fo-onen realm and its management of colonization), and sought to enable it constantly and to guide it in such ways which promised a fortunate development for the future of the folk, while "false wisdom" — *modern morality* — generated only hypocrisy through misunderstood inhibition of the natural laws of evolution and guided the natural instincts along unnatural pathways because they will not inhibit or even suppress these. If Wiegand von Theben, the pastor of Kahlenberg (already by his cover-name) has shown himself to be solidly connected with the Kahlenberg, formerly known as Zeizoberg (Mons Celius) and in the legends as well — which are too numerous to mention or interpret here — and to be completely bound up with this thing, then one has to be necessarily impelled toward the conclusion that this Wiegand von Theben cannot possibly have been a "singular personality," that the name was not a personal name but rather had to be the name of an office that belonged to a whole long series of interconnected individuals — much like the title "pope," "king," "grandmaster," etc. —who through the long course of centuries had taken this artful edifice of concealment (*Verkalung*) into the High Holy Tribunal (*Hohe Heimliche Acht*) according to ancient well-tested Skaldic and Armanic rules, for such a prodigious deed would exceed the abilities of any single individual. One of those from the long line of "Wigands" may have been the "jolly councilor," *id est* "court jester" of the Merry Otto, although, of course, no documentary evidence can be brought to bear on this, since those who took Armanism into the High Holy Tribunal probably had more than one reason not to let their exalted secret be drug through the archives as the burden on the back of a dead donkey using colorful, elegant writing, for they knew of a more fitting preserver of their secret knowledge which they could surely expect to reveal it at the proper moment in time, and this true assayer is none other than— our dear German mother tongue itself.

Therefore when those, such as the previous "Wigands von Theben, the Pastors of the Kahlenbergs"[18] had taken the old Armanic *situlih* into the High Holy Tribunal, and — yielding to the predominance of the flow of those times — to transplant their true wisdom by means of *Kala* into more receptive times, unfolding their high art they were derided as "jesters" or at best "jolly councilors" by their own contemporaries, so it did not go a hair's breadth better or worse for them than for those related to them in conscience and spirit as fellow sufferers in the present-day who people meet with the same sympathetic smile as they deem them crazy or at best people who do not deserve to be taken seriously. The ancient Armanic *situlih* will therefore likely have to be preserved for an even more distant future which will hopefully be able to understand with better insight and finally be able to recognize the *situlih* as the true culture and put away the lax morality of today into a temporary and finally permanent junk gallery for the history of negative culture with all due regard.

If all that has been said about the *Kaland*-Brotherhoods and about the Pastors of the Kahlenbergs is brought together, and if one considers that these reports come from relatively late times, from the years 1220 and 1337, at a time when these institutions were already coming to an end, while their time of origin has to lie as far back as at least seven to eight centuries earlier, this means that the transition from Wuotanism to Christianity was no sudden thing and in no way can it be seen to be concluded by the mere common baptism of the inhabitants of a certain strip of land, but rather it proceeded very slowly and nowhere was it brought to a complete conclusion, but rather it usually fell into a faltering pattern and solidified in incomplete stages. Furthermore, however, there is the key as to how the teachings and customs of Wuotanism were melded with those of Christianity over the course of time, a work of art which was actually the task of those

Kalandars and their schools, and the articulation of which served the system of *Kala* which was sufficient to establish this transition in teaching, custom and cult in both word and meaning.

A piece of evidence for what has just been said that should not be underestimated, and something that brings more to the report, would be the letter by Pope Gregory I, the Great (590-604) which he wrote to Abbot Mellittus of Canterbury in which he said:(c) "Tell Augustine[19] to what extent I am convinced after long observation concerning the conversion of the English: that the idolatrous churches of these people should not be destroyed, but rather just the idols in them should be destroyed and the buildings sprinkled with holy water, altars built and relics deposited in them. Because those churches are well-built they should be transformed from the service of idols to the true worship of God, so that the people, when they see that their churches have not been destroyed will sincerely lay aside their error, recognize the true God and all the more happily gather at the places they are used to. And because the people were used to slaughtering many oxen at their idolatrous sacrifice, **this custom also must be turned into some sort of Christian celebration**. They should make huts out of the branches of trees around the former idolatrous churches on the day of the consecration of the church or on the memorial days of the holy martyrs whose relics are to be placed in their churches, to celebrate the festival day with religious feasts, no longer to sacrifice to the Devil, but rather to slaughter them for food in praise of God, thereby thanking the provider of all things for their sustenance, so that they, while some external joys remain for them, become all the more fitting for their internal joys. Because to cut off everything suddenly from crude minds is without doubt impossible, and because also the one who wishes to ascend to the highest level gets there step by step, but not by leaps to the height."

These few words explain the complete plan as to how, from the Roman standpoint, the transition from Wuotanism to

Christianity was aspired to and achieved, until other means came into active use. This basic Christianization plan was not only valid for Britain, but rather formed for the foreseeable future the guiding principle used by Christian evangelists in all countries and, of course, in Wuotanistic Germany as well.

Therefore, conspicuous similarities are also found in the articles of faith as well as in customs and in the legends of the Catholic Church as compared to the teachings, customs as well as myths and tales of Wuotanism and its mythic personification, no less in the annual festivals, their names and numerous other customs. That was, however, in no way the work of the Christian evangelists, but rather the work of the Armanic *Kalanders*, who, after they saw that the evangelists would succeed, established with them certain forms and names on a completely scientific basis in order to preserve, even if in the new form of the Christian religion-system, the *Wihinei* of Armanism and kept it alive. Therefore, we see everywhere *Kalands* composed of priests and laymen, men and woman, for originally it was those — if the expression is allowed — members of the "Wuotanic priesthood," which consisted of men (Armanen, Skalds, Bards) and women (Albrunas, Hag-Idises, Walas and soothsayers). Christian priests, in the beginning the Roman apostles themselves, were in a certain sense students, and only with the passage of time did the *Kalands* become purely Christian brotherhoods, after the Armanic traditions had been suppressed. Therefore, the Catholic bishop is always himself the head of every *Kaland*.

Right away the comparison of the Christian to Armanic and Wuotanic conceptions of divinity and its triplicy provides the first piece of evidence for the Kalandic art of synthesis. The widespread erroneous perception that the teaching of the triune nature of God was transmitted to the Germanic peoples through Christianity and its Roman evangelists is not accurate, for — as we already know[20] — the primevally holy triad in more manifold aspects than was present in Christianity was actually known, and was an original property of the Armanic *Wihinei*. With reference to what was said in the third volume of the collection *Deutsche Wiedergeburt* (German

Renaissance) concerning the Religion of the Aryo-Germanic Folk, etc., it should be remembered that the Great Spirit, the unknown and unnamed God, as pure spirit, was not revealed, but in its first emanation (first Logos, the God-Soul) All-Father is the creator of the worlds. In his second revelation, as the Earth Spirit, he is Wuotan, who was also called the All-Father, insofar as it concerns the gods and humans of our terrestrial system. In relation to the All-Father, who created the worlds, Wuotan is, however, his son. After the dissolution of matter into pure spirit Wuotan too, like the All-Father, goes back again into the *Ur* and both are again one in Surtur, the spirit of salvation. This triad is once more found exactly in the Christian three-foldedness, God Father, God Son, God Holy Spirit. In that scripture, it is also proven how — as in the propagation of plants — every member of an Armanic triad in language, order, belief and custom results in a subsequent triad. Thus, rooted in the second level of divinity, the second Logos, in Wuotan, the further triad *Har-Jafnhar-Thridi* or *Wuotan-Donar-Loki*, which encompasses our sensory world, and this triad is again found in the Christian tradition in the Three Holy Kings to which we will return later. Concerning this, it is just to be remembered that in the case of each of the triads explained here (with only two exceptions that will be justified later) the third entity is always portrayed as being black in order to indicate the Dark, the Mysterious quality of the *Ur* or the primeval condition, for the first entity is a symbol of arising, the second of becoming and the third that of transformation or passing away to a new arising, therefore a symbol of death.

The divine masculine Threeness correlates to the threefold nature of Mary in Christianity. But since Christianity only recognizes one God in the Trinity (*Dreifaltigkeit*: "Three-folded-ness") but otherwise no other "gods," it has to replace these with *angels* and *saints*. Now in order to better understand the mother of Jesus whose name in Hebrew, or better said in Aramaic, was Marjam, and who was honored by the Roman Christians to a much higher degree than a goddess, but still only as Saint Mary, which was something conceptually nearer to the feeling and meaning held by the Wuotanists who had gone over to Christianity which is indicated by the name Maria in and of itself, a name which is purely Aryo-Germanic and according to the stem-words [ma-ri], means "increaser of generation," which was reinterpreted as "increaser of grace." Egyptian Ma is likewise Aryan as is the Indian Maya; today the Swedes still call the mother of Jesus Maja [pron. ma-ya]. In Bavaria, the folk-legend, or better said a folk-belief, is known having to do with the three Moja [Maja], by which is meant the three Marys, which in the memory of the folk does not refer to the triad in the cult of Mary and not to the three Marys of the Gospels, but rather to the three Norns. Also, they live on in legend, myth and folktales as the Three Sisters, Three Daughters, Three Virgins, Three Nuns, Three Countesses, Three Queens, etc. In all this secular folk-belief is actually indicated whereby not superstition, but rather the further developed ecclesiastical faith under the influence of folk-wisdom is indicated; the mother of Jesus was also introduced into the order of the Wuotanic triad, thus this happened very intentionally from the purely ecclesiastical, dogmatic perspective and actually corresponded perfectly to the Armanic triple level according to arising, becoming and transformation (passing away to a new arising). These three special groups in the cult of Mary are discernable by the characteristics of Mary: as the Virgin Mary (Freya, Ostara) and Mother Mary or the Mother of God (Frouwa, Frigga) and as the Sorrowful Mary of the Black Madonna (Fria, Helia). This threefold cult of Mary corresponds point by point to the triplicy of nuns and most especially to the Mystery of Frouwa or Frigga in their triads: Freya-Frigga-Fria or Freya-Frouwa-Helia, which can be determined from their auxiliary or sacral signs, attributes or hieroglyphs. These plainly speaking sacral signs are to be found here alongside the Virgin Mary there with Freya, such as the moon, the serpent whose head she treads under foot, the white dress and blue gown, with the Mother Mary, as a symbol of her maternity, the Christ Child, the red dress and the gown of blue color, always a sign of Frouwa or Frigga; with the Sorrowful Mother of God, the Black Maria in ancient images with a black cloak, the corpse of Jesus on her lap as a remembrance of the Dark Helia or Lady Death, Fria; only relatively younger representations also show the Sorrowful Mother of God in a blue cloak, as the ancient mythological memories had already faded. Mary — as a goddess representative of death — is also repeatedly represented as a Moorish woman of black skin color with an equally black child in her arms; as on the famous miraculous image of Czenstochau, as seen in the images of grace in Alt-Oetting, Brünn, Vienna and in other places, and thereby fully brought into the cult of the goddess of death, which **generates children and fruits in abundance and therefore alone possesses the right to give and take life.** As a result of this last reason there is also the folk-understanding with regard to judgment and appreciation of the miraculous power of a pilgrimage-image of Mary, the "Black" Madonna, above all others with the presupposition that the greatest power is ascribed to this one, to liberate tormented humanity, who flees to her, away from all the miseries of the earth. The popular understanding, strong in faith, judges with a resolve which is intuitively correct in the Wuotanic sense, for death alleviates all sufferings of the human body because it thereby liberates the soul from all that. Surely death has to come as a gift from the divinity if it is to function as a blessing; voluntarily chosen death (suicide) is a curse, for it encroaches upon the intentions of the course of fate without knowing what it is and destroys the effect of salvation, turning it into mournful effects of mischief.

    Just as in pre-Christian Wuotanism where the All- or World-Spirit All-Father receded behind Wuotan-All-Father and as the Solar-Spirit receded behind Thor the Storm- and harvest-God— back into darkness, since to the people this divine personification appeared conceptually closer to them as the helpful, and therefore more important, divinity— in exactly the same way we see this in Christianity where the image of God-the-Father is pushed back into the darkness and in his stead God-the-Son, or Jesus the Savior or Salvator, comes to the foreground of divine worship. Now it is important to see how the image of Jesus in the depiction of the Gospels was fit together with the Wuotanic feelings of the Germanic peoples. The condition of this adaptation was, of course, the function of Jesus on Earth, thus it could be said his historical activity depicted this in a way intelligible to the Germans, brought it more into line with their sentiments and formed it in a way that would seem not all that foreign or exotic to them. The first one in Germania who undertook this assignment was the Old Saxon *Skop* (Skald), who started out using the skaldic type of Armanic heroic song, but as he grew older withdrew into a monastery and composed the *Heliand*. Without doubt he was a *Kalander*, something about which we have already written extensively. Commissioned by Ludwig the Pious he undertook this assignment and created a folk-epic completely in the style of the familiar heroic songs intended for performance at folk-gatherings in order to channel skaldic poetry into Christian contexts. Therefore, this poetry too rests — completely in the sense of *Kala* and the kind of work of the *Kalanden* — upon a broad Wuotanistic foundation in many cases permeated with purely Wuotanistic mythological elements, and Jesus himself is conceived of and portrayed in this manner. The residence of Hel is hell, spirits of affliction are living beings, even the Norns appear, and a dove sits upon his shoulder on the occasion of his baptism, just as the two ravens sit upon Wuotan's shoulders. So, feeling his way from within the folk-soul, using external signs in a conscious way, he translated the story of Jesus from the Oriental milieu into the Germanic one, out of distant antiquity into the time of his contemporaries and fellow countrymen, and at the same time also the landscape and the customs of the Near East to those of his North German forested lowlands. But the forest-land [G. *Waldland*] is no longer the "Asiatic ruler-land," [G. *Waltland*] but rather the realm of the Devil; so, every place, whether large or small, is a fortress, whether Bethlehem, Rome or Jerusalem. The shepherds to whom the angel announced the birth of Jesus are tending the horses. Jesus himself is a military king entirely within the Germanic cultural context, he is a prince, ruler, lord, "the mighty Christ," and his disciples are his retainers. Everyone connected with him is a hero, thane, knight, and where he speaks to the people according to the Gospel, the savior rules as a rich king who proclaims his will as such. The relationship between the Savior (*Heliand*) and his disciples is that of a king to his retainers, and that of each of them to him is that of a vassal whose highest duty is loyalty in service. But they only fulfilled this duty with very imperfect results, and making this conceivable to his Saxons, as proud as they were of their loyalty as retainers, caused the good *skop* a great deal of difficulty; but he knew a way to express it and says: "It was not only simple fear that caused them to abandon the one Born God; it was already long since determined by the Words of the Prophets that it had to turn out that way, therefore they could not avoid it." Also, the denial of Jesus by Peter was painful for the *skop*, something he could only excuse with difficulty due to his loyal Saxon heart, although he also says here again, "that Peter did not have control of his words, for it was to be meted it out, by the one who watches out for humankind here in the world,"(See Song 59) and then grants that Peter was probably overtaken by fear and his courage weakened; but here the *skop* saves himself through the representation of the painful regret with which Peter mourns his situation in order to let the mysterious judgment of God rule in the end, a judgement that always leads us humans through the greatest of sufferings toward salvation; and thereby God wanted to teach Peter in order to set him up as the highest prince over his house. Upon his own forgiveness that he experienced after this deep fall he was to learn clemency when he, as that highest prince, was to rule humanity mercifully to provide atonement and forgiveness. To this end, his own experience is to lead him to this recognition, for "no power is found in the mind of men without the power of the Lord, and therefore let each guard himself against pride (= self-aggrandizement)." But earlier the *skop* had portrayed Peter as a bold warrior who had intervened for Jesus with a sword in his fist. In this portrayal,

the joyously fighting Saxon skald can be recognized for whom it is not sufficient that Peter cuts off the ear of Malchus; no, the blow would have to be performed better than that according to Saxon custom, for the head is split and the cheek and ear split to the bone, and blood gushes out of the wound.
— And then there is how he describes Jesus himself: In his childhood, he is already a "dear little man," the mightiest of men, yet he remained silent on this description, his Jewish origin is downplayed as much as possible [the monk Otfried also neglects mentioning this; about this more later] and he likewise no less conceals the entry into Jerusalem with Jesus mounted on an ass, which seemed far too far-fetched as an animal for a king for our honorable *skop* to mention to his Saxons. He has Jesus gather his band of disciples, for whom he is their generous, kind prince, the most powerful of men, their lord, who is the best and kindest of kings and sons. He fulfills great signs, redeems man from the worst sufferings that demons have hurled against him, gives the poor sustenance and drink, promises powerful protection for the coming times in his kind teaching, down from the highest mountain peak as shepherd of the land, as lord of all people. But the small royal crown offered to him by Israel, is rejected by him, it is for him, the lord of all peoples, whom he actually created, too limiting.

But just as the *Kalender*-skald suppresses or alters events drawn from the circumstances found in the Gospels, he does the same with regard to the teachings of Jesus, if he is apprehensive about these not being pleasing to his people. Thus, he leaves indications regarding divorce unmentioned, because he knew that they did not fit with Germanic views. As he prudently knew as much to preserve his fellow countrymen from such teachings as turning the left cheek to the one who struck you on the right, or relinquishing your coat to someone who desires it, or even recommending the love of one's enemies. He also left out the part of the Gospel in which Jesus challenges the disciple to follow him without, as the man requested, first having to bury his father who had just died (Mat. 8:21-22), for this demand was too contrary to Germanic sensibilities. Morally this *Kalender*-skald tried to teach the Germanic folk a new sort of heroism that saw its highest exercise as the overcoming of one's own lusts, the fulfilment of consecrated teachings, charitable action, devout work and the patient endurance of one's fate. And therefore, he puts forward the "suffering Jesus" as an example worthy of imitation. Therefore, Jesus is shown bravely approaching his suffering and death. So he ameliorates the psychological pain of Jesus in the Garden of Gethsemane in comparison to how it is shown in the Gospel; nevertheless, he does also portray the distress of Jesus, but the words: "Father let this cup of suffering pass away from me, etc." is not spoken of in the *Heliand* in awareness of his divine majesty, instead the *Kalander*-skald has him say: "May men not be otherwise saved, and if I must leave this dear life of the children of the people in terrible agony, then Thy will be done... Pay no heed to the wellbeing of my flesh, for I shall fulfill Thy wise will." (See Song 57.) And the cross, which the Germans did not yet know as an instrument of death, he simply called the gallows, as the place-name "Golgatha" simply means "station of the gallows."(d) When, in spite of this, the *skop* reports the call of lament of the one hanging on the cross ["Why hast Thou forsaken me!"] he is in no way trying to make his listeners believe that Jesus feels that he is "god-forsaken"— which to him, to a priest of Armanic *Wihinei*, had to appear incomprehensible— but rather according to his conception this lament had to do with the situation that Jesus felt himself to have been "forsaken by men," by which the poet, sure of his effect, was striving and aiming to instill the highest form of success. In a just as exalted manner he also portrays the mother of Jesus as the most beautiful of women and she alone seeks the young Jesus [Luke 2:48] in the Temple among the scribes, while Joseph remains unmarried and is not mentioned at all. And thus, the whole story of Jesus is elevated to a higher, more illustrious level than the everyday world of men, just as every person is so honored who works in the environs of the lofty king, and this magnificence is transferred to the scene of these events, for Egypt is he joyous green meadow, the most gracious and noble ground and the Nile the most splendid of rivers.

A contrast to the poem of the *Kalander*-skald of the *Heliand* is provided in the form of the Gospel-Book [*Evangelienbuch*] of the monk Otfried from around the same time which belongs to the last third of the ninth century, which has the same goal but pursues different means. If the author of the *Heliand* was a skald and as such a *Kalander*, then Otfried was a monk, a scholar in the Roman-ecclesiastical sense. He worked on his Gospel-Book as a Roman-ecclesiastical scholar and not as a folk-poet, and even if he — as a Ripuarian — made use of the German language, which he had mastered at a level commensurate with his education, even as the first to use end-rhyme in certain passages, he has certainly already distanced himself too far from Wuotanism as well as Germanendom to be able to speak to the folk in the way that the poet of the *Heliand* could. Also, he, the Ripuarian, was certainly no *Kalander*. In spite of this, as a Rhine-Frank, he wants to glorify his own folk in whose Frankish language he wrote, and places them on the same level as the Greeks and Romans. Otfried is, however, no poet, but just a scholar. His depictions are always derived from sermons and become weary due to their stereotypical exegesis and use of the Bible and the Gospels. Because he was not a *Kalander*, he avoided all connections to Wuotanism. But in his *Gospel-Book* even Otfried portrays the action in a way entirely accommodating to contemporary Frankish circumstances as they relate to the people, their values and customs, and as regards landscapes and locations. After all the Germanic blood is still enough alive in Otfried, the Ripuarian, monk so that he, in a way similar to the *Kalander*-skop of the *Heliand*, finds it necessary with certain events in the Gospels to accommodate these things to Germanic sensibilities; but he does this as a theologian, not as a skald. He has the disciples flee because they were unarmed, and a whole army was opposed to them; and Peter is unarmed, fighting for his lord and master pressed in the midst of armed men, but to no avail, and this is supposed to ameliorate his later denials of Jesus.

That Jesus, as God, withstood the temptations of Satan is for Otfried not so difficult to explain: Jesus is actually God, his humanity is only an appearance, but as such the monk Otfried entirely misses the concept of temptation. If Jesus is God himself, able to produce bread in an instant, who owns the entire world anyway, what is that stupid Devil thinking with this temptation?! If the Devil had known who Jesus was, he would have left off with the temptation, so Satan did not understand how Jesus could be without sin as a man, and how he was able to remain without sin in this world of sin. Satan was still hoping that appearances could deceive him and therefore attempted the temptation. Since Otfried himself did not understand the human nature of Jesus as a God-Man, and still only saw God himself in Jesus, he cannot conceive of the spiritual struggle of Jesus in Gethsemane, how could God have such doubts? Therefore, he leaves this event unmentioned. And this manifestation of divinity in Jesus and the humanity of the son of God that is considered to be only an external appearance, or covering, finally also leads Otfried to the conclusion that the words of Jesus on the cross: "My God, why hast Thou forsaken me"? does not, in a way similar to that in the *Heliand*, refer to an inner God-forsakenness, but rather to the outer human-forsakenness. Otfried, too, leaves out passages he finds questionable, just as the poet of the *Heliand* does, and does this to a more wide-ranging degree than the skald, and it can be seen how the theologian went to work with much more cunning calculation than the more courageous skald who ventured to say much more than others ever dared to. The difference between the two works of poetry is clear: The *Heliand* is a folk-poem intelligible to everyone, while the *Gospel-Book* is a learned poem meant only for theologically educated circles; while the *Heliand* poet conceals himself behind his work and behind his heroes in a completely impersonal way, the poet of the *Gospel-Book* stands beside his heroes preaching and dogmatizing. The thing the two poems have in common is the heroism of Jesus as a folk-king for his folk, for whom he brings victory through his death.

The comparison of these two poems about the same subject, on the one hand by a *Kalander*-skald and on the other by a Roman-ecclesiastic dogmatist, clearly shows how Wuotanism and Christianity blended together into a mixture; but by this example the seeds of the coming second phase can be perceived, one that the Ripuarian cleric with his Roman inclinations began to enkindle in that he nourished and promoted the Ripuarian-Frankish desire for domination borne in the Ripuarian spirit and thereby conjured the second bloody era of the transition from Wuotanism to Christianity which will be referred to later in the course of this work.

* *
*

The same correspondences are found between Wuotanism in the exoteric sense as well as the Armanic *Wihinei* in its esoteric understanding, and the legends of almost every ancient saint of the Church and in the customs of the people who honor them. Very noteworthy in this respect is the legend of the "Three Holy Kings," about whom the only source [Mat. 2,1] says nothing of their names, or their number, or their royal titles; there is only mention there that they are wise men (magians) from the East made up of an indefinite plural number. Only later was their indefinite plural number developed into a triplicy, and their names appear as well, and now that they had been defined, the were transformed into the three wandering Ases "Wuotan-Donar-Loki," and so the title of king was ascribed to them since people were able to believe that gods could be humanized only in the form of kings. Their names are therefore also Germanic, which are Gastibor, Melichari and Balthasahar, which have been reduced down to the familiar forms Caspar, Melchior and Balthasar.[21] It is significant that in this triad too the third is thought of as a black figure and is portrayed as a Moorish King, that is, once more as the Dark One symbolizing death. The Day of the Three Kings leads into *Fasching* in Catholic countries; but this is nothing other than the ancient Aryan festival of the origin of humanity. The name of the festival, *Fasching*, is based on the *ur*-word *fa*, expressing origin, generation, making, etc., and the other *ur*-word *ing* which means "descendants"; so that the concept *Fasching* simply means "generation of descendants"; *Fasnacht* is the night of generation and *fas-ten* is the cessation of generation. This great festival of the origin of humanity that is linked to the great festival of the origin of the All with the holy night of Yule in its midpoint, stands opposite the equally holy festival of passing away as a lead into the festival of rebirth, that the Church celebrates as "All Souls" and "All Saints." And here the obstacle is revealed that the *Kalander* would not be able to avoid and which brought the calculation of Church festivals into such inconsistency.

In spite of the fact that the day of the birth of Jesus was unknown in primitive Christianity, this ancient, pre-Germanic Christianity accepted as his birthday as well as the day of his death as the 25th of March in the symbolic exposition of the words of Christ who called himself the Alpha and the Omega. The first evangelists of Roman Christianity in Germany now attempted — as already mentioned — together with the *Kalanders* — to reconcile the Christian festival calculations with those of Wuotanism as much as possible in order to coordinate the three holy times of Wuotanism with the Christian festival times and they executed this work with admirable intelligence as well, right up to the day of the death of Jesus, which, according to Wuotanistic festival calculation, would have to be postponed to the Festival of All Saints as the memorial of Wuotan's sacrificial death ["I know that I hung on a wind-cold tree, I myself consecrated to myself"], but this would have contradicted the specific assignment, that the death of Jesus was to take place before the Passover festival in Jerusalem. By this means it was mandated to celebrate the festival of resurrection of Ostara, at which time Wuotan returned to the world of humanity together with his disembodied souls out of the underworld, which was simultaneously the great festival of death belonging to that divinity. Christ rose up from death after three days in the Wuotanic sense as a victor over death, but the mystical death celebrated during holy week intrudes in the midst of the bud and bloom of youthful life, whereas the holy week celebrated during the time of All Souls and All Saints would have achieved the most powerful effect. Then the mystical ring would have been closed. Instead of this, the forced arrangements that can only be made to fit with difficulty, is noticed by everyone. So, we see the birth of Jesus, the young Sun-God, on the 24th of December (Winter Solstice) and the conquest of death through the return of life in spring, i.e. by Wuotan's return with his army of souls for rebirth, that is the resurrection of the dead, Easter (Day of Spring and equinox, Ostara); here Christianity could only fill this gap with the festival of the Annunciation of Mary and celebrate the resurrection of Christ as the overcoming of death. In order to remain true to the Gospel, the Ascension of Christ had to be included before Pentecost occurs, while this would be celebrated at the time of the Summer Solstice and not in the middle or beginning of May. Probably, the festival of Pentecost corresponds in time and name to the Wuotanistic festival calendar as the Christian festival of the "outpouring of the holy spirit," but in spite of this it could only partially substitute for the marriage of the Earth Goddess with the Rain God, especially the outpouring of the holy spirit which appears in the form of fiery tongues, was able to substitute for Wuotanistic views only in a forced manner. In any event, John the Baptist is now celebrated at the summer solstice instead of Baldur and the Ascension of Mary (Freya's Heavenly Ride) is celebrated as the birth of Mary on the 8th of September. Here the equivalence of the celestial virgin [♍] and the ear of grain [Freya, Isis, Ceres, Astraea] is made manifest, who once more appears three weeks later with a scale [♎] in her hand. St. George [Serpent] is celebrated at this time during the Spring Aequinoctium, so too is St. Michael [Dragon], who once more holds the scales, like Forsetti at the Mihilathing, during the Autumn Aequinoctium. Now comes All Souls and All Saints, the sacrificial death day of Wuotan— but the Church could only celebrate the collective festival of death, and had to divest itself of everything divine as it was compelled to shift the deep mystery of this to the Easter-tide.

Now, if this melding of the Christian festival calendar with the Wuotanistic calendar was only an incomplete one as a result of unavoidable difficulties, then the arrangement was an almost artistic one in its details, which ought to be examined here in its general features.

Each of the three great main festivals: Holy Night (Origin), Ostara and Pentecost (Becoming), Solstice, All Souls and All Saints (Transition, Passing away to Regeneration) was further divided into three parts each of which symbolized unto itself Origin, Becoming and Changing and by means of a time period without festivals — to some extent indicating the "primeval condition" — which prepared the way for the next festival time.

Thus, the main festival of the year, the Great Festival of Origin that we know as "Holy Nights" [= Christmas], demonstrates its preparatory festival of origin, its main festival time and its post-festival time, and the first of the preparatory festival times can be recognized on the 23rd of November when the ancient runic calendar begins winter on this day and with this day also the Hilling-month begins.

In order to organize the following presentations more clearly and to give the necessary explanations briefly in just a few words, it has been decided to arrange things in a calendrical form and order it schematically.

Festival Calendar of the Hilling-Month
A. Preparatory Days

23rd of November, Leaf-fall. Clemens. *Kala* of the name *klem*, "force"; *men* = "man";[22] i.e. "man of coercion" = Winter-giant, death. — Legend [the code-words written in bold-face type]: "With an anchor around his **neck** he was thrown into the sea." *Kala* of the legend: **Anchor** *an* = "by, in, with"; *kar* = "enclose, tight," i.e. "tightly **enclosed**"; neck [G. *Hals(e)*] *hal* = "hail"; *se* = "sun; solar salvation." Sea = *lagu*; **law**. — **Marble** [G. *Marmor*]: *mar* = "more, increase" *mor* = death: Increase in death. Church: *kerke* = *kar* "enclosure"; *ke* = "can," strong [G. *stark*]: "strongly enclosed; closed up, dungeon [G. *Kerker*]. — Interpretation: "The coercive man

[Winter-giant, death] tightly encloses the solar salvation through the law of increasing death in his prison [church = dungeon]." The runic calendar begins with Clemens' Day, the winter and places the anchor beside the bow of Uller. Uller, the ever-transformative spirit [God]; bow = *ybe* – *aub* = *uff* = owl = ghost [spirit] or Divine Knowledge. The Winter-giant is represented here by *St. Clemens Romanus* according to *Kala*.

25th of November, Leaf-fall. Katherina. *Kala*: *kat*, "struggle"; *rein*, "pure" [G. *rein*]: Pure fighting solar lady, sun-lady, sun-goddess. — Her wheel is the sun-wheel, the solar cycle. Therefore, she is called upon to have the sun shine and for the rain to pass. Rules of weather: 1. "Katherine suspends the fiddles, then the weather should be fine," 2. "However the weather is on Katherine's Day is how it will be next January." 3. If Katherine protects us from frost, then we'll long be wading through damp and dirt." 4. "Katherine suspends the fiddles and flutes." [Advent, see below.]

30. November. Leaf-fall. Andreas. *Kala*: *an* = "by, in, with"; *dre* = "turning, spinning, transformation, changing"; *as* = "opening, governing, beginning"; *an-dre-as* = "At the beginning of the change of governance," therefore = Beginning of the month of Hilling [= Hilling = healing: "month" = *man* = "moon," *noth* = "need" = "coercion: the coercion of the month."] The sanctification of Andreas-Day begins on the previous evening, as folk-belief ascribes to him the power to effect great changes in all life-situations. Therefore Andreas-Night is one of those nights in which a person has a free question to fate [G. *Shcicksal*]. It is celebrated like the nights of smoke/incense [G. *Rauchnächte*], when spirits roam free, although it is not counted as one of these nights.

1. December, Hilling-month. Eligius. *Kala*: *El-li-gi*: *el* = "divine fire, primeval fire"; *li* = "light"; *gi* = "to give"; i.e. "the primeval fire, God, will once more give forth light." — The legend and its *Kala*: "The horse of Eligi was made lame by a witch. Eligi removed the bewitched foot from the body of the dapple gray, and re-forged a new healthy foot, and replaced it on the gray, and pinched the witch's nose with his

red-hot tongs to punish her." The Kalic interpretation is: "The gray steed of the light-bringing fire-god [Wuotan] Slider [Sleipnir] is lame because the time of his rejuvenation has not yet come. The lame foot [*fos* = generation] is restricted origination and becoming in nature; the pinch of the nose, the removal of that restriction. For this reason, "Eligi" is the protective patron of smiths, namely the cure-smiths for horses, and Eligi-day is the festival day of smiths.

4. December, Helling-month. Barbra. *Kala: Bar-bar-ra*: *bar* = "life"; *bar* = life"; *ra* = "to bring forth." — "Bringing forth all of life." This is the ancient Aryo-Germanic cult of the Norns and of fate [G. *Schicksal*] here kalically Christianized. The Nornic triad is Christianized as the three holy virgins "Barbara, Margaret and Katherine." Bound together in the following proverb: "Saint Barbara with the tower, Saint Margaret with the serpent, Saint Katherine with the wheel are the most beautiful maidens in heaven." These symbols, i.e. tower, serpent and wheel are, however, kalically interpreted as follows: "tower" = "turn, spin" = "arising" and therefore Urda, the first Norn. Serpent, i.e. dragon = *du* = "there"; *ra* = "to bring forth, generate," *ka* = G. *kein* ["none"] = "cessation of generation." Margaret, however, tramples the dragon's head (as does the Virgin Mary and Saint Gereon, i.e. Geryon = "return," etc., i.e. removal of the restriction on generation, that is, liberated becoming or Verdandi, the second Norn. — *Rad* [wheel]: *ruoth*, "rod, raw." The wheel has three interpretations: 1. Sun-rise, birth, growth, ascension, etc., 2. Course of the sun, right, governance, becoming, etc., 3. Sun-set, court, death, death leading to rebirth, to submerge, decay, rot away, etc., and therefore it is the hieroglyph of the third Norn, who holds court, called Skuld [G. *Schuld* = guilt]. The dried-up staff stick of Pope Urban which he shows to Tannhäuser when he said to him that he could no more forgive him of his sins than this dry staff would ever be able to become green again, but in spite of this it did indeed sprout greenery. This dry staff is the Barbara branch that is sold at all churches as an oracle of the re-greening of one's luck.

6. December. Hilling-month. Nicholas. *Kala: nik* = "decline, sleep, death"; *ol* = "spirit"; *la* = "life"; *us* = "out": "The death-sleep of the spiritual life has ended," spiritual life returns. Therefore he comes riding on his white horse, and so the horseshoes of this white horse are walled up in Nicholas churches and his sacrificial pastries are in the form of horseshoes and are called *Kipfel* [little wagon-posts] or *Beugel* [croissants] for this reason Nicholas is the patron saint of Alpine associations and brotherhoods, because he, as the returning Wuotan, breaks the power of winter, and similarly he is also the patron saint of sailors since he makes the streams and seas ice-free as the father of the nixes, Nikuder.

13. December. Hilling-month. Lucia. *Kala: lux* = light. According to legend she was thrown into the fire because of her faith, but it could not harm her, because the light cannot actually burn up the sun. This fire is, however, *Wafurlohi*, the fire of death [cremation] that glows around the *Hindarberg*, the death-mound that of course destroys the soulless bodies but cannot harm the incorporeal soul, the light. It is the *Wafuhrlohi* that glows around the bed of Brünhilde and through which Baldur [Siegfried] passes on his steed Grani at which time it is extinguished. The twilight skies of the morning and evening are its symbol, which glow every night around Walhalla [the realm of the dead] as the "strong grating" which protects the gods from attack by the gigantic powers— or materiality. Lucia is accordingly the lady of the sun, she is Brünhilde, the slumbering solar-bride of Siegfried. "Saint Lucia makes the light stop short."

17. December. Hilling-month. Lazarus. *Kala: La-za-rus*: "life-generation-coming forth," i.e. "life pressing toward birth wishes to come forth." The seven [*Niedelnächte*] begin preceding the Holy Nights [Christmas] as a pre-festival week [*nid* = "grudge, envy, restriction"; *el* = "divine fire," *si-bi-un* = "solar distress"]. These are the seven nights in which the sun fights for its rebirth against the curse of death [Urban], a battle in which humans are supposed to help the sun out. Symbolic foods as hieroglyphs: *Nidel* = "curdled cream; noodles, a flour-food," have the same meaning and the same reference

point as sacrificial foods as *Nidel*; poppy = |G. *Mohn*| = warning |G. *Mahnung*| |from moon, lunar appearance, *mananen, mahnen,* "warn"|, noodle = *Nidel,* therefore warning of a grudge, and so poppy-noodles are also a holy food before and during Holy Nights. Therefore, the poppy-mortar is used as an oracular instrument for the drawing of lots, because it is sanctified by its use as a tool for the preparation of holy food.

18. December. Hilling-month. The Church celebrates the commemoration of the expectation of the birth of Jesus by Mary. The ecclesiastical relation of this memorial-day to the Wuotanistic "Nidel-nights" is evident, an intention which becomes more obvious in Advent. Advent: The ecclesiastic time of preparation for the birth of Jesus. There are four Advent-Sundays, because there is a teaching about the fourfold arrival |*Adventus*| of Jesus: 1. Into flesh; 2. To death; 3) To judgment; 4. Into the heart of humanity. The fourth Sunday and Wednesday before Christmas is called "Rorate" upon which days the song "Tauet, Himmel, dem Gerechten..." is sung.(e)

Kala: ad-vent = "on the turning" — *Ro-ra-te*: "right-origin-generation"; therefore "At the turning of perpetually generated rights." Symbolic holy-foods: *Rorate*-sausages: ancient sausage = primeval origin; in connection with *Ro-ra-te*: "Primeval origin of the arising rights," therefore: "The eternally immutable God-Spirit in the newly won form of appearance." — Advent-sow: Swine = *su-ine* = *uinnen* = winning, good luck; sow = *sa-afa* = "generating product"; G. *Ferkel* (piglet) *uarchel,* i.e. *uar, or* = descendant; *ach* = "to bring forth"; therefore = "increase of descendants, of the blessings of marriage." So the concepts of the good-luck pig, the good-luck sow and the good-luck piglet therefore are connected with sacrificial and sacred foods. Children born on the first Advent Sunday will be able to see spirits, i.e., be talented as mediums and clairvoyants. The three Thursdays of Advent, also called *Klöpfelnächte* |Nights of Little Knockings|, *Anklöpfnächte* |Door-Knocking Nights| also occur in some localities at the same time as *Gebnächte*

[Giving-Nights] and other special local festivals, such as *Burenklas* (*Bauernklas*) [agriculural], *Frafastentier* [relating to goblins] and similar ones, all of which would lead us into too many details than can possibly be explained here.

B. The Main Festival Time and its Secondary Festival Days

The *Raunächte* [*Rauh*-nights](f) and Twelfth Night. Seen from the perspective of all the other pre- and post-festivals of Christmas, the most important of the accompanying and auxiliary festivals are the so-called Twelve Nights and the *Raunächte* that are closely connected with these, all of which establish for the Hilling-month that unique and special position among all other annual festivals, but which are still too little appreciated and even remain almost ununderstood.

The Twelve Nights break down into two halves and in the six days[23] from the 25th to the 30th of December the other six days from the last to the 6th of January. The 31st of December (Sylvester) therefore does not belong to the Twelve Nights, for it is the "Rift in Time," which as the *Now*, as the *Present*, symbolically terminates the *Ur*, and ushers in That Which is to Come, so it divides the spiritual or divine from the religious or secular, the past from the future and simultaneously reconnects them. For this reason, all pre- and accompanying festivals up to and including the 30th of December are sanctified to the sixth day of the twelve memorializing the generation of the world by materialization of divinity, that is, the *Ur*, of the mystical past, while all following festivals after the "Rift in Time" are made holy to the *generation of humanity*, that is, to the future. What is written here will become clearer as the four *Rauhnächte* are examined and considered in more detail in that the first three of these are sanctified to Ur in the well-known three-level division, and the fourth is called upon to inaugurate the future. The first three *Rauhnächte* fall between the 20th and 21st, the 24th and 25th of December and the 31st of December and the first of January, while the fourth *Rauhnächte* falls between the 5th and

6th of January. Through the high sanctification which they have in common they prove the special holiness of those festival days which precede them, but indicate their own sacred meaning through the particular cult attached to each individual *Rauhnacht*.

The first *Rauhnacht*, or Thomas Night, celebrates the great mystery of the generation of the young Son of the Sun, that is, the arising to a new being of the Sun and at the same time of the All and of all life. The well-known customs and attitude of the folk connected to Thomas-Night are easily explained based on his interpretation.

The second *Rauhnacht*, the "great Mother-Night" or the true Holy-Night, is a celebration of the great mystery of the Birth of the young Son of the Sun and therefore his being, becoming and rulership, as all of life in the All, which is not difficult to recognize in popular customs and attitudes.

The third *Rauhnacht*, the Sylvester Night, which is directly connected to the oft-mentioned "Rift in Time," is related to that transformation toward a new arising, to the ascension of divinity into human existence (the third logos) as in the life of the All, in the eternal transformation of which it takes part in the idea of the eternal transformation, in the idea of eternal rebirth in the uninterrupted becoming and passing away to new arising of this form constituting eternal *being*. Therefore, the third *Rauhnacht* stands directly on the border between the divine and temporal, between the *Ur* and the becoming of the future, on the "Rift in Time," to effect the shift of the divine manifestly into the consciousness of humanity. The gods stand behind us as the *Ur*, as the old year, the new time, the future, lies — as the year that has just begun — in front of us, prepared by the gods who direct the future as the power of destiny, which we ourselves — as Germanic folk — are able to shape. We are called upon, as assistants to divinity, to perfect the work of creation, and the Earth, given to us as a place to reside — Mitgard, Manheim — as our own to finish out, making it as habitable and comfortable as possible. In the process of eternal rebirth we were our own ancestors, just as we will be our own descendants, and therefore as our descendants we eternally reap the happiness and misfortune according to how we, as our own ancestors, have succeeded or failed in our attempts toward both good and evil. This is the teaching of passing away toward a new arising, of the development of *Garma*, which the third *Raunacht* expresses symbolically and so establishes the certainty beyond all doubt that in the All no death exists in the sense of a complete annihilation, rather we live eternally conscious as ourselves within divinity as its individual rays, eternally without beginning and without end, only subject to the transformation in the apparent forms of our essence (personality).

The fourth *Raunacht*, the Gi-Perahta-Night, belongs to the future and to Mankind in logical recognition of the meaning which this fourth night offers. It is sanctified to the living Perchta, and therefore leads into *Fasching* [*fas-ing*], that is, the festival time of the "generation of mankind" which follows the festival time of the "arising of the sun-god" and the "generation of the All" [creation of the world]. — The name "*Raunacht*" is derived from neither *Rauch* ("smoke") nor from *rau* ("raw"), but rather from *Ro*, that is right, salvation and designates that exalted concept of Aryo-Germanic knowledge about salvation and law, which unifies in that one word, *Rau*, both heavenly and terrestrial law and every kind of salvation, for Armanism, just as its religious system (Wuotanism) synthesizes at the innermost level knowledge, action and faith so that the Aryo-Germanic person not only knew what he believed, but rather that which he knew and believed was manifested in his actions such that his *Wihinei* was not merely professed as doctrinal opinions with empty words, but rather they were also confirmed in the full measure of that word through his actions and inactions in life. *Rau*-nights distinguish themselves as oracle-nights[24] as follows: On the Thomas-night (also Andreas-night) the question of fate is simply "whether?"; on the holy-night "who?" and on Sylvester-night [New Year] "how?", while on Perchte-night no further oracle questions can be answered, for it, i.e. the time ushered in by it, is supposed to actualize the steadily increasing oracles of the first three *Rau*-nights.

21st December, Hilling-month: Thomas. First *Rau*-night. Kala: *tho-mas*: *tho* = "doing"; *mas* = "share, measure," etc., therefore "action according to measure" or "share in the action." What this is trying to say will be shown with reference to the celebration and will be even clearer when one considers that the designation "mass" in connection to the Catholic offering service is derived from this same *ur*-word, *mas*, and not what is usually said (in an intentional effort at confusion) from the exclamation: *concio est missa* ("the assembly is finished"). In the English word "Christmas," that *ur*-word, *mas*, is still used in the same sense, and therefore does not mean anything like "the mass of Christ" in the modern understanding of the word, but rather logically "sharing of the Christ," and it has the exact same meaning in the words "officers' mess," messmate and other similar designations for the expanded entitlement to a share, such as, for example: Leipziger Messe ("Leipzig Fair").

24th December, Hilling-month, Adam and Eve. Holy Night. Second *Rau*-night. That the celebration of the first human couple is concurrent with the "Great Mother-Night" of the All proves that this night was not only from the ecclesiastical viewpoint consecrated to the memory of the birth of Jesus alone, but rather once more to the arising of the entire universe is being emphasized. Here Adam and Eve are representative of Ask and Embla [Ash and Alder] the first married couple, whereby we are automatically directed to the Aryo-Germanic cult of the tree and forest, to which even today we ascribe the origin of the customary holy-night [Christmas] tree as the "tree of Christ." Everyone knows the quaint figure of the ice-grey little man with his snow-covered cowl who carries a felled pine tree in his arms as he appears to us at Christmas-time though our windows smiling at us in a friendly manner, but few know his name; they are satisfied just calling him the "Christmas man," because they do not know that he represents the revenant Ase, Vidar, who comes forth from his forested abode as a herald of *rebirth*. The forested abode is, however, the land where the Ases rule, because the salvation of arising lies in the forest and the Ash too is a forest-tree— the tree of rulership [G. *Waltungsbaum*]— even as the Ash is the symbol of the first created man. And the nine kinds of wood or trees, which constituted the fire-mothers, or kindling, on the altar slab, out of which the tenth — the ash!— engenders the initial spark of the first flame is the fire-father, all others too are forest-trees, and the ninth on the altar slab was the Fir [G. *Tanne*][25] [*tanne* = "doing-bearing"]. Everywhere when we look back into far away mythic times of the Aryo-Germanic world, we will soon confront the holy forest— the divine realm!— the Aryan tree-cult. From this comes the ancient Germanic, pre-Christian, custom of placing a fir tree in front of the gate to friends' houses on Christmas Eve, hung with thoughtful gifts, decorated with lamps of life. But the father of the house also puts just such a tree in front of his own court-yard gate as an offering to consecrate it to the gods who pass by outside. Out of these two traditions the custom of the Christmas tree was developed, which in the end had it being brought in from its location in front of the gate to a place within the hall, which it today still occupies and hopefully it will retain this place forever into the future. It is an error to insist that the Christmas tree can only be traced back to the seventeenth century simply because it was understandably never mentioned before then, because when it was first mentioned it began to arouse anger as being a "heathen custom," which is due to the fact that it had just come into the sphere of observation and became an object to be described in writing. At the same time, it took on a Christian meaning without ever having to change its innermost essence. — The "Fire from nine-kinds of wood," that plays such a prominent role in this second *Rau*-night, only here receives its complete explanation as the generation of the holy Christmas [*Weihnachten*]-fire on the altar-slab.

25th December, Hilling-month. Christ-day. *Kala: Heiland*, i.e. *Heliand*. Esoteric meaning: *hel* = "hidden, concealed";

iand = "the other," i.e., the other Solar-God, that is, Froh or Baldur are concealed in him. — Exoteric meaning: *hel* = "death"; *iand* = "turner, changer, conqueror"; i.e. the conqueror of death in the Christian sense. Since the *Kalanders* could not harmonize the story of the life and sufferings of Jesus with that of Baldur, they designated Jesus as the Heliand, [26] to wit, the "concealed Other-one," and alongside this other Sun-God was caused to rise up a new Sun-Hero, to whom they transferred the divine myth in humanized form to the latter, along with the *Wihinei*, and took them into the *Hohe Heimliche Acht*. **This is how the heroic sagas came into being.** For this reason, we see along-side the Sun-God *Badur*, the Sun-Hero *Siegfried* developing, and all the other gods and goddess of the Ases and Vanes, etc., are humanized in saga narratives, while the divine myths slowly appear to be forgotten. All of these heroic names, however, conceal divine names, such as here will be demonstrated with one example. Baldur, formed from the *ur*-words: *bal-da-ur* can be analyzed as "sun-to-*ur*," and Siegfried is formed from the *ur*-words *si-gi-frid*, analyzed as "sun-going-death," both names therefore speak to the mythic theme that all sons of the sun will certainly have an early death. Christ-day, or Heliand-day, celebrates the young sun-god as a child, that is, in his arising phase, in both Christianity and Wuotanism.

26th December, Hilling-month. Stephen: *Kala: ste-fan: ste* = "stand"; *fan* = "generate," that is: "standing generations," or "life that stands up again." Yesterday, Baldur or Froth [Froh = Lord [Herr], the Glorious [Herrlich] was still a child, today he has become a man and is ready for battle. He mounts his steed in order to ride into that battle. Everything that is told about the horse of Baldur, Froh, Wali or Phol appears to have been transferred to Stephen's horse, although he, in keeping with Christian legend, could never have anything to do with a horse. For this reason, he is made the patron saint of horses and the church celebrates the oat-festival [*Heferweihe*]. In St. Pölten in Lower Austria during the Middle Ages an oat-tithe was paid, which was called the *Wuot*-feed. Wuotfuator, i.e. Wuth-father, to wit, storm-father is, however, a byname of

Wuotan, and this oat-tithe was a sacrificial offering to the storm-god of old, but which was later transferred to the church.

27ᵗʰ December. Hilling-month: John the Evangelist. *Kala: jo-hans: jo* = "fire"; *hans* = "Ase, ruler," that is: "the fire-ruling Ase, the Judge, the Transformer." Baldur has conquered the winter- or death-giants and the Ases prepare the funeral pyre for these. Standing opposite the water-baptist, John (24ᵗʰ of June, Brachet) is the fire-baptist, John, just as the lind-serpent (water, George on the 24ᵗʰ of April, Oster-moth is opposite the dragon (fire, St. Michael, on the 29ᵗʰ of September), for the victorious water (ice) is winter, death, while the victorious fire, which thaws the ice, is life. But since the God of Salvation always becomes the God of Damnation, and the reverse is true also, fire is also death when it turns water into steam (it spiritualizes it!) just as coldness brings back life when it condenses the steam into water in the clouds. (Spirit is materialized, and demonstrated in the case of the First Logos.) But the effects are not the same, because while fire leads to spiritualization as death, water leads to the most rigid materialization as death (ice), which however, sooner or later still has to yield to the fire of spiritualization. Therefore, the decision maker or judge is in all cases the spirit of fire, the *Urfyr*. Therefore, today on the third festival day the reborn Sun-God is the one who turns everything toward new-arising, the judge, the purifier, who baptizes with fire. For this reason, the regular Thing [legal assembly] fell on St. John's Day, so it was a court-day. Here might be a place to mention a characteristic example that is not directly connected to our present subject matter, but which nevertheless clearly demonstrates how *Kala* was used in the in the interpretation of customs in order to preserve Armanic wisdom under a Christian cover. This wisdom is this: "Six weeks (*sex uaken* = sexual activity, arising) and three days (*tritac* = generational activity: becoming) has to have laid a wagon wheel (*uagenrad* = working rightly, i.e. right-doing) in the bed of manure (bad situation, sleep of death), that is thrown into the fire (*fyr*) and the "court session" could only last as long until the time when the wheel and hub (bearer of birth, i.e. the navel) became ashes (*ask* = arising; ash = symbolic holy sign of regeneration, from this originates the custom of imposing ashes on the faithful in the church on Ash Wednesday). The *kalic* interpretation of this symbolic custom is: "Arising, becoming, turning toward passing away led to the sleep of death, but the *Urfyr* causes the one being born to a new resurrection." To this the Yule-Wheel is also deeply connected: Yule = "spirit," *rad* = "right, salvation, etc."; therefore: The right spirit, spiritual salvation and the concept of *julen* ["to celebrate Yule"] = to spiritualize action from materialistically mundane action.

28th December. Hilling-month. Innocent Children. On this day Wuotanism, like the old church, committed a bloody mysterium with real human sacrifice, actually child-sacrifice, sacrifices which had, however, already been replaced by substituting offerings of bread by pre-Christian Germans.[27] In the Church, the so-called compelling mass was celebrated as just such a sacrificial mass, which was, however, only celebrated for the inner grades of the mysteries, and otherwise kept strictly secret. It was only at the time of the Reformation that it was stopped, although it is historically provable that it continued up until the time of the French Revolution as the "Black- or Devil's Mass"— in the context of "Black Magic." Cologne had its own cemetery for innocent children, relics from there are actually those of the "Three Holy Kings," which are the remains taken from such sacrifices, as the skeletons of these "saints" have been proven to have belonged to children no more than six years of age. For present purposes, this short reference should suffice.

31st December. Hilling-month. New Year [Sylvester]. Rift in Time; the Now; Third *Rau*-night. *Kala: sil-fes-ter: sil* = "target, goal" [G. *Ziel*]; *fes* = "to generate"; *ter* = *tern, tarn* [*tarnhut* = "cap of concealment"] = "to conceal," therefore: "the aim of generation concealed [*verkalt*]." The Rift in Time divides and connects *ur* and *ur*, to wit, past and future, through the *Now*, for this reason the tool that indicates the Now is called the *Uhr* [clock].

1ˢᵗ January. Hartung: Telemachos. *Kala*: *tel* = "earth"; *em* |*am*| = "mother"; *ak* = "working"; *os* = "mouth, opening; to come forth," therefore: "the Earth as Mother causes [the production of new life]." Therefore, the Self-congratulation for new beginning; the eating of fish [*fi* |*fa*| = "generate"; *isk* |*ask*| = "arising," therefore: to cause to arise; to begin" the eating of "sow-snout" [the plantain herb] [28] (See Advent); ginger-bread tents [G. *Lebzelten*] (= *leeb* = "life"; *zel* = *sal* = "hail, salvation"; *ten* = "to hold"), therefore, "the holding onto the *Heil* of life, health"; the drinking of mead [*meoth* = *me* = "increase"; *oth* = *od* = "spirit"; increase of spirit, stimulation] to increase the spirit, etc.

2ⁿᵈ January. Hartung. Makarius. *Kala*: *ma-kar-ri-us*: *ma* = "increase"; *kar* = "enclosed"; *ri* = "to grow"; *us* = *os* = "mouth, opening, to come forth"; therefore: "The still enclosed increase [the harvest, yield, winnings, etc.] will grow forth."

3ʳᵈ January. Hartung. Genovefa. *Kala*: *ge-no-ve-fa*: *ge* = "giving"; *no* = "bearing"; *ve* = "generating"; *fa* = "generating"; i.e. "The Giving, Bearing, Manifold-Generating," to wit, the All-Mother Earth. The Earth-Goddess [Freya] who transforms herself from her winter form [Fria, Helia, Chrimhild] into her summer shape [Frouwa, Brunhild], transformed from the Death-Goddess into the Solar Bride and Goddess of Love, who appears concealed in the legend of Genovefe, in which her whole myth is masterfully hidden. As the Earth-Goddess, who has again been received by her groom, the Sun-God, she is Nehalenia [*ne* = "bearing"; *hal* = "salvation (G. *Heil*)"; *en* = *an* = "by, to the, etc."; *ia, je* = "time"] in her wagon-ship [*kar* = "car, wagon"; *naval* = "ship,"] who is in the carnival procession— therefore: "The salvation-bearing of the nourishing[spring] time", which introduces the general time of generation, carnival[29] [second interpretation: *kar* = "contained"; *ne* = birth"; *ual* = "of all," therefore: "She who inducts the 'contained All-birth' of her essence." As such, she was much worshipped, especially as a Goddess of Protection from base entities, which she then retained in concealed Christian form as a patroness, as for example in Geneva, Paris and other places—Yet she is not Peratha [Berchta] herself, but rather only her harbinger.

5th January. Hartung. Telesphorus, Fourth *Rau*-night. Giperahtanaht, Perchten-night. *Kala: tel-as-pho-rus*: *tel* = "earth"; *as* = "mouth, opening, coming forth"; *phor* = *fyr*, ur-fire, sun"; *us* = "mouth, opening, coming forth": therefore "The divine solar fire opens the earth for production." Since, however, as has been said already, after the mysteries of the divine have been celebrated, the mysteries of humanity are commenced, the festival of divinity appearing manifest in humanity [revelation of the Third Logos], thus this night served as the introduction of a new time, such that the coming day is also called the Great New Year.

6th January. Hartung. Epiphania, Three Kings, Peratha. The high festival "divinity within humanity entering into revelations" [Third Logos] was concealed in the festival of the appearance of Jesus among mankind" [Titus II.11] concealed under the name Epiphania, a name which means nothing other than "to generate descendants"(g) in its *Kala* which corresponds with the name and *Kala* of Fasching, as was shown above. The Three Holy Kings festival was covered earlier, and here only remains to mention their star, about which is constructed the kalic formula: *tri kunig steor*, which is interpreted: "in the turning (of time) generation returns." An addition to this would be the expansion of the kalic interpretation of their gifts of homage, to wit: frankincense [*rökels*], myrrh [increase, G. *Mehren*] and gold [*or*], which results in: arising, becoming and *Ur*, to wit, the passing away into *Ur*, or if one takes *or* for the descendants, the interpretation would be: arising and increasing of the offspring. Likewise, other names for the Three Kings(h) are: Ator = "impulse, arising"; Eatar = "return"; and Peratores = "prepared descendants" are of symbolic importance, when one considers that on this day the Ases, both male and female — the divinities of life — recurrently effect their entry. Perahta, the splendid [G. *Prächtige*] is the weaving-, the spinning-one, in modern German, Bertha. Today she sits on her festival day behind the altar in Our Lady churches and spins; the hum of her spinning wheel can be heard, but she is invisible. In spite of the fact that Christianity tried to replace her with Mary the Queen of Heaven, she could not be banished from the churches, and she had to be tolerated behind the altar that had once been consecrated to her, and in spite of this she still possesses it, even if under a different name, for she is and remains Perahta, the splendid, the queen of heaven, the increaser of all that rises up, of all graces.

C. After-Festivals and Concluding Festivals

7th January. Hartung: Valentin. *Kala*: Valentin, Wiland, Volund, Uoland: *vol* = "spirit"; *and* = "the other": "The Other Spirit," to wit, the Aryo-Germanic God taken up into the *Hohe Heimliche Acht*; therefore, Junker Voland was made into a name for the Devil by Christianity.

20th January. Hartung: Fabian and Sabastian. *Kala*: *fa* = "generate"; *bi* = "by"; *ian, jan* = "time: gestation period." — *se* = "sun as (feminine) generator"; *bas* = "house-holder"; *ti* = "holding"; *jan* = "time: house-holding time"; i.e. after the festivals going back to taking care of the house in order to increase its blessings. Therefore, in folk belief it is heard: "Sebastian takes the first cut of the last cake," i.e. the festive times of feasting are over, now work begins again.

23rd January. Hartung. The Wedding of Mary. The return of increase — distributing divinity is interpreted by the Church in this way.

25th January. Hartung. Conversion of Paul is symbolically related to the conversion of the Germanic folk, so that a Saul should become a Paul.

The actual conclusion of this festival period is again formed by three days, which are Rose-Monday, Fasching-Tuesday and Ash-Wednesday. Rose-Monday, named after the secret rose [*rosa mystica*], the archaic symbol of union, was the day for engagements, the bridal purchase, and Fasching-Tuesday served as the day of marriage. Other customs are also connected to Fasching-Tuesday which recognize it as Fasching-Thing's Day, that is, Fasching Day of Court. Of the numerous customs relating to this only two will be introduced here. In Cologne it was customary to entertain the "old maids," called Möna[30] locally, during these days, when satirical pastries were served to them, among which the well-known "nun-farts" or "wind-bags" could not fail to be present. The concealed meaning of the name of this pastry indicates in this circumlocution something like "a useless thing." In Vienna, the custom still exists that is practiced annually with the Fasching-Tuesday-Processions involving carrying along a replica of the spire of St. Stephan's cathedral on a wagon in the parade that real splendid shapes of old maid-type satirical figures appear to be cleaning with wash and rubbing sand. Laughingly it is still said that: "**On Fasching-Tuesday the old maids have to rub (scour) Stephan's tower.**" Why this has to take place, however, no one knows, and the investigation of this "why?" never occurred to anyone until now. This too is pure *Kala* which preserved an alternative tradition in the concealed double-entendre of the code-words, behind which lie hidden an esoteric interpretation covered by the exoteric meaning. The code-words in that ancient Viennese tradition are: "Fasching-Tuesday - old maids - Stephan's tower – rub"; i.e. translated in reverse: *Fasing thingstag mönas ta fa thurn ri ban* and means: "A day in court for procreation, non-procreating ones preventing continual generation cleansed by death." This points to a court of procreation that existed in ancient times that condemned those incapable or procreation to death, since the production of fit offspring was considered a duty in the service of God. As time went on, the death sentence was done away with, but those unfortunate ones became dependent to a level that bordered on slavery in that they were stripped of all of their human rights and were viewed and treated as mere inanimate objects. From such circumstances of contempt there resulted the minimizing expression for a person in a grammatically neuter word in German: *das Mensch*, which is an insult [*das Mensch* = "wench, hussy, slut"]. The situation is, however, noteworthy in that such folk-beliefs, folk-tales and folk-customs always cluster around old churches and cathedrals, and this is because all ancient churches, to wit, cathedrals, emerged from Halgadoms of Wuotan. They also all have their devil-legends, for the Devil is a generator as well, who had his sacred space in the cathedral, and it would be Christianity that changed the light Solar-god into the dark Prince of the Deep [Depths]. And here is discovered the esoteric interpretation of the rubbing of Stephan's tower by the old maids: "All of life in arising, becoming, turning and passing away to a new arising is divine, therefore each and every restriction is devilish, and therefore the first is the *Good*, the latter *Evil*, and for that reason all those who are infertile, whether man or woman, should be destroyed, in order to make room for the fertile ones."

To Fasching-Tuesday also belong all legends and customs that have to do with *Minne*-castles [Halgadoms of the Lady, in Christian times: Our Lady Churches], the "Courts of Love," Fen-hills, etc., as well as the legend of the Fenussin [Lady Venus in the Hörselberg and in other Venus Mountains of which there are three in Lower Austria alone, which are even today called "Venusbergs" on maps.] The legend of Tannhäuser begins on Fasching-Tuesday and ends on All-Saints, but all of the legends can only reveal their true meaning by means of *Kala*.

Ash-Wednesday was the ancient *Asken*-day, that is, the Foundation Day of a new household, of the young couple who had just been married the day before, therefore *ask* = "arising." Today the Church conducts the imposing of ashes, which is carried out before the main altar, in which the priest makes the sign of the cross in ashes on the forehead of the devout believers with the words: "Man, Thou art of ash and to ash shalt Thou return!"(i) This is once again *Kala*! Ash [*ask*] in the third word-level means "destruction" but in the first level "arising," for there is no such thing as destruction, rather only a passing away to renewed arising. And the cross is even today the old sign of increase [+ = plus, more] and so the priest speaks the truth, for behind his words which are meant to remind us of death is hidden the esoteric meaning which says: "Man! Thou art from the Ash(-tree) [Ask = ash-tree, the first man, Yggdrasill = World-Ash, Tree of mankind, Tree of Knowledge], art Thyself an Ash, wilt always remain Ash through the sign of life, the cross!"

† †
†

Due to the limited amount of space allotted to our present study, it is not possible to outline the other festival times as thoroughly as the festival times for the arising of the gods, the All and humanity; it should only be mentioned that they were all transferred under their old Wuotanistic names into Christianity, where they as much as possible accommodated the Wuotanistic forms and norms. Thus we still celebrate the *Os-tar*-festival [*os* = "mouth, opening, arising," with reference to *as* = Ase, in the spiritual sense; *tar* = "turning, generating in a material sense," therefore: inception of the renewed life of earth through the solar-divine force of generation from Mother Earth] appears under the ancient Armanic name, although Christianity does not celebrate a divine marriage, and even inserted a death-festival out of necessity in order to celebrate the *resurrection* as the festival of victory over death. Just as with Pentecost, about which I have already spoken. I have only to add here the consideration of a few very special festival days in their concealment under *Kala*, since in connection with this we will turn our attention to the expressive symbols (attributes, hieroglyphs) in the sense of *Kala*, which appear to stand in very puzzling relationship to the corresponding pictorially represented saints. So, on the 21st of October the festival of Saint Ursula is celebrated, which the folk quite correctly speak of as Sint Ursula (not Saint); that too is *Kala* and means "eternal primeval-ness" [*sint ur sala*]. Saint Gertrude, who was called upon throughout the Middle Ages by dying people for a grant of the "blessed [*salig*] condition (*Urständ*), is depicted with a staff with a mouse running up its length. The *Kala* means: mouse-staff [*ma-us-sta-fa: ma* = "increase"; *us* = "out" [G. *aus*]; *sta* = "standing" [3rd word-level, therefore "standing still"]; *fa* = "generation": that is, "cessation of generation," i.e. "death." For this reason, the mouse is a death-animal, i.e. an animal which portends death. The *Kala* for the meaning of the name Gertrude or Gertraut [*gere* = *kere* = [G. *kehre*] ("turn back"), *traut* = "turning," which cancels out the death symbol, for this name means: "return," therefore "rebirth." Gertrude is, therefore, the female conductor of souls through the primeval condition [*Urständ*], through the condition of death between dying and being reborn, just as Sint Ursula with her 11,000 virgins, are the mothers of the future. The numeral 11,000 is also *Kala*: *einliftusunt*: *ein* = "the One, God";[31] *lif* = "lope, run, life"; *tusunt* = *tusen* = "enclose, conceal"; therefore: "the divine or spiritual life [hidden in the *Ur* or primeval condition]." The same is true of Saint Gereon [*ger* = *ker*; *ri* = "arise, grow"; *on* = "man, the man of recurrent arising"]. As shown above, a protective patron of rebirth, as are many others, e.g. Moritz, Kastor, who promote development and thereby obtained for themselves their "own treasure of the soul." To this is again directly connected the Christian belief in the resurrection of the flesh as well as the condition of blessedness (community of the saints). The surest way to attain the state of blessedness is through martyrdom — as the Church and Wuotanism both teach — which leads directly to a union with God. Both religious systems, however, also think that the "self-sacrifice" of an effective life is one that does not shrink from aspiring toward, and recognizing, every form of suffering, persecution and renunciation, even up to enduring death without making any cowardly compromises or objections; whether this death ends up being on the battlefield or on a scaffold. These blood-witnesses, which the Church calls martyrs and Wuotanism calls Einherjar, are among the "community of saints." It was only later misunderstood — whether in Wuotanism or Christianity — that only death on the battlefield or a martyr's death was required to attain this state, whereas this state is not the only absolutely necessary capstone of an entire life led in a condition of sacrality or in the grace of God as a form of continuous self-sacrifice. The condition of sacrality, or being in the grace of God, simply consists of one consistently promoting the good with feeling, thoughts and actions within one's own sphere of power, and of abstaining from, or preventing from occurring, whatever in a bad sense tries to restrict development. Whosoever attunes his actions and abstentions to these concepts, and defies all enmities courageously, thereby sanctities his life as a self-sacrifice to divine intentions, and therefore stands in the state of divine grace or sanctification, and enters — even without a martyr's crown — into the realm of divinity upon death. Only later did more recent Christianity continually darken the teaching of the resurrection of the flesh, which today is restricted to the Last Judgment. But these matters lie outside our field of consideration here, although they might just be mentioned for the sake of comparison, that peoples who believe — or better said know! — this and cultivate the idea of reincarnation are invincible, because they know that they will be their own descendants and therefore also know that they will exist in the future as they are preparing for it in their present actions and abstentions and so they will never dare speak the ugly phrase "*après nous le deluge!*" ("After us the deluge!") The attitude of the Japanese in the last East Asian War [Russo-Japanese War, 1904-1905] and their successes showed, to the amazement of the Christianized Germanic world, what power that knowledgeable belief in rebirth was inherent in the Japanese, a belief to which they still today adhere. **They simply do not fear death, because they know that it cannot kill them, for they will be reborn.**

The "straw-death," or better said, the *straw-life* which is meant by the "straw-death," is the opposite of heroism in life, whether it leads to martyrdom or battle-death or not, for it can also end in a slow death by starvation which this humane present-day age causes through the withdrawal of every necessity of life from those uneasy spiritual heroes (because today heating fuel is just too expensive!). Mistakenly, "straw-death" was thought to mean death in a sick-bed, which is wrong. A "straw-death" is a death at the end of a uselessly squandered life, for "straw" = *stra*, is "empty, hollow, sterile," and since such a squandered life is likewise sterile and empty as straw is, this is also a death, and therefore: straw-death. Those therefore who die a straw-death do not go to Walhalla as Einherjar, nor into heaven as saints or blessed ones, but rather will be reborn according to circumstances which will force them to lead heroic lives in order to attain the state of sacrality, which each person must eventually attain, since Armanism does not acknowledge the idea of eternal damnation. The promised joys of heaven or Walhalla as well as the sufferings of the other abodes of departed souls are realized during the next incarnation and even during the course of several of these here in this world of humanity in renewed human bodies, but not as a reward or punishment, but rather as the effects of self-created causes according to immutable garmic laws.[32] Therefore, the Christian heaven, the Christian purgatory and the Christian hell are to be sought and found here among us, the living, as well, without being tied to outward splendor or outward misery.

From everything that has been presented up to this point, although by far it has not brought out everything completely, which would actually require more content than can be offered in these pages, it is nevertheless comprehensive enough to offer a picture of how in the time of the era of Christianization the messengers of Roman Christianity, united with the Armanic *Kalanders*, were concerned with guiding the religious system of Wuotanism over into the other system of Christianity and melding the two together on the basis of the *Wihinei* of Armanism. It was shown that those Germanic people who undertook this task in the form of a brotherhood called the "*Kalander*" combined and outwardly — for all appearances — were joined to Christianity, but inwardly they took Armanism into the High Holy *Acht*, indeed, it is obvious from many signs that the lower Armanic grades, and from ancient custom even the common folk, also cultivated the religious system of Wuotanism in secret as heresy or superstition, and only outwardly called themselves Christians.

Now it was not only those Armanen functioning as *Kalanders* alone who therefore continued to cultivate Wuotanism in secret, but rather also other Armanic groups did the same thing, each according to the aspects of their special functions, so a great deal of attention will have to be paid to these here in order to survey and understand the interactions within the whole institution.[33]

The Armanen were also arranged in the three groups according arising, becoming (being) and transmuting (passing away to a new arising); and formed the Skalds (first), Heralds (second) and the Femanen, the third ordering group (not level or degree), each group of which had its own three-leveled division according to grades of knowledge. The *Kalanders* are therefore to be reckoned in the strict arrangement to the third group in the order, to the *Feme*, for they had the court, judgment [G. *Richten*] (*Roden*) to take care of, i.e. to guide the process of transition, although, as already indicated, all groups and sub-groups of the *Armanenschaft*, each in its own way, take part in these processes equally. The Skalds are concerned with spiritual things: with language, poetry and science. The heraldry with the graphic arts and the art of governance, and the *Femanen* with the law and courts. Accordingly, we recognize in the *Kalander*-Skalds those poets who poetically revise, according to the rules of *Kala*, the myths of the gods and heroic legends and shape the necessary new names for the "Germanic-Christian cult." The heraldry, as *Kaland*-heralds, likewise create according to the rules of *Kala*, pictorial works, be it on the shields by the heralds who make the coats-of-arms or other pictorial works (as painters), be it in works of architecture (as builders or carpenters), be it in plastic works of stone (sculptors), or of wood (carvers of images) as they likewise had to conceal in *Kala* the Wuotanistic representations behind Christian appearances. Finally, it was the *Femanen*, as lords of the *Kaland*, who cultivated the Aryo-Germanic *Rita* and preserved it in the High Holy *Acht* the Aryo-Germanic peoples long before the Roman (in)justice, that which came to be expressed in the formula that the count of the *Feme* (G. *Femgraf*) spoke at the opening of the Thing: "I bid the just and forbid the unjust." Since he was bidding Aryo-Germanic law, however, he was forbidding the Roman Law, which he characterized as "unjust." In this rank, the "*Kalanders*" worked for a few hundred years longer and built up in common with others that admirable artistic construction in which the old teachings appeared in new clothing almost unchanged, and the whole renovation would have been completed, if another violent and bloody era of Christianization had not broken out during the eighth century— the aim of which was to root out the remains of the cult of Wuotan violently with fire and sword, with torture and the headsman's ax.

Where earlier there had existed peaceful mutual work through which — entirely in the sense of the letter of Pope Gregory I the Great (590-604) shown above — certain Halgadoms had become Christian Cathedrals or churches or cloisters, and the Roman clerics had been unified with the *Kalanders* in a common work, there now commenced violence instead of interaction, the Halgadoms — which were usually very rich — were confiscated by the princes,|34| and in the structures left behind usually monasteries were established. The Armanen who remained loyal, fled or hid themselves — in the countryside — if they did not die by the executioner's hand, the Halgadom-schools, some of which were entitled to be called "high schools" |universities|, a name which they also bore, and which exalted them in the sense of our universities of today, were closed and all of Germania was systematically de-educated, a process about which I thoroughly reported in my work about the *Armanenschaft* of the Aryans. What were the few monastic schools with their paltry Latin lessons supposed to mean, the only function of which was to supply needed clerics?!|35| Those Armanen who remained loyal to the *Rita*, as well as to Armanism, withdrew themselves back into strictly exclusive secret organizations, which had their cardinal points in the *Kalands* as long as these remained secure, although in these they were also forced to preserve their secret behind outer Christian forms with the greatest of care, and finally in addition — let the Pastor of Kahlenberg, Eulenspiegel and others be remembered — they might be publically active under the cap and bells of feigned foolishness. In the *Feme*, which was kept completely free of Christian influences, they now had their final basis, but this too fell to Christianization when the Archbishop of Cologne, as Duke of Westphalia, procured for himself the superintendence over the *Feme* in the 13th century— as a Ripuarian! But Armanism still glowed under the ashes; the Armanic Skalds still lived and worked in the secretly cultivated Skaldic Order, likewise in the old "lodges," as in the secret leagues for the "heraldic guilds."

It is instructive to examine somewhat more precisely than has previously been done those secret places of refuge taken by Armanism in order to survey, and be able to evaluate, their meaning and continuing function right up to the present day. According to a guild-legend of the master-singers of Nuremberg, that certainly reports the full truth even if it has only been transmitted as a legend into our times, tells of "twelve old masters" who made a request of Emperor Otto I to allow them to perform the master-song in the *ancient* form. The emperor referred them to the pope, who summoned them, rejected their request and commended them as heretics into the living fire. In these "twelve old masters" we can, without doubt, recognize Armanic Skalds, who probably hoped that Emperor Otto I, as the first Saxon emperor, would be well-disposed toward them after the Frankish, or Ripuarian, dynasty[35] of Karl the Great, the Saxon-slayer [*sclactenaere*] had lost the rulership of Germany— but this was a hope by which they were certainly deceived. In spite of the surety of such a beginning, at the time such a move was not openly possible for the Saxon Otto I due to political reasons, but nevertheless the Skaldic Order continued to blossom concealed in the High Hidden Institution, but it also had taken on outwardly Christian forms, but inwardly it continued to be animated by the Armanic spirit, and later it emerged into the public sphere as the Christianized Oder of *Minne*-Singers. The old Aryo-Germanic heroic songs were preserved by this order in the High Holy Institution, for otherwise the old heroic songs would have emerged concealed in Christian form. Now the era of the great national epics began, there arose the *Nibelungenlied* and the *Gudrun* and many smaller epics, all of which without exception appear as ancient Wuotanistic heroic songs in Christian form. How else but through guard and care within the High Hidden Institution would it have been possible to cause all of this very ancient material to appear again so suddenly, as there had elapsed centuries between the original composition of this material in the form of heroic songs [belonging approximately to the fifth century] according to their origin as revisions of the even older songs of the gods? Through more than six hundred years these heroic songs, derived from ancient songs about the gods, originated secretly and were perpetuated orally, just to have them rewritten in new Christian forms! But the authors of those great and small epics were still masters of the art of *Kala*, for these now Christianized ancient Wuotanistic heroic songs that arose during this era turn out in many parts to be intelligible only by means of Kalic interpretation and reading. A few appear to be pure nonsense without such an interpretation, as for example the *Rolandslied* (Song of Roland) or the song of Lohengrin, (The Knight of the Swan). The first is the exact opposite of what people up to now understood about it, namely it is not a panegyric to Karl the Great— the Saxon-slayer, but rather a call to struggle by the *Feme* against him, and Lohengrin is no less than a song praising the *Feme* in which we find out that Walther von der Vogelweide was the grandmaster of the *Feme*. The literal meaning of the words is deceptive! How could *Minne*-singers — who were also knights!! — have allowed themselves to enter into a competition in which the loser would have to end his life in humiliation at the hand of an executioner on a scaffold?! — And because the *Feme* was the last vestige of the Aryo-Germanic *Wihinei*, Aryo-Germanic *Rita* and Aryo-Germanic justice, the ancient faith of Wuotan and the new Roman church religion are embodied together, and as such encoded (*verkalte*) persons are placed in opposition to one another. The outer meaning of the words is secondary, only in the conceptual meanings contained in *Kala* is the core revealed, which was intended for men of knowledge. The mastery of the poet in handling *Kala* was demonstrated in that the outer sense of the words was formulated such that it all appeared quite believable. The song of Lohengrin is an apprentice-level work, one which would not have been possible for master-singers who would have handled the *Kala* more skillfully. But just after the completion of the prodigious spiritual creation known as *Minne*-song it quickly began to decay, or just as it was apparently blooming its demise had already been completed and its successor, the Master-song, was already being suffocated by formalities even before it was born. Nevertheless, individuals did struggle through the centuries — misunderstood and mocked — and struggle on into the future — as sympathetic wretches or ridiculous idealists — in order to carry their spiritual treasure over into a more beautiful brighter future. They were just born to early, but they will be reborn as the masters of the future! Hail to them, to their own future, and to our own! —

That which concerns the builders' lodges as that other Armanen-group, which took *Armanism* into the High Hidden Institution and at least transmitted their misunderstood symbols and isolated, equally misunderstood, teachings down to our times, requires that a position has to be taken against the enormous errors regarding the observation and presentation of these symbols right from the beginning onward. The letter of Pope Gregory I the Great [590-604], already mentioned above, speaks of heathen or idolatrous churches as if they were solid permanent buildings, and an early medieval poem contains the representation of a heroic battle in which the skald uses the following depiction: "You know well how there is hacking when Woldan [Wuotan] hews his church doors" to describe the sword-work of his warriors in a very visual way. These, and yet more similar pieces of evidence, reliably prove that the Germanic folk were already building wooden and stone structures earlier than the sixth century, and ancient ruins of walls at the sites of fortresses and sanctuaries going back to the times before the beginning of the Common Era, and which are found in regions where the Romans never came, provide evidence that the Germanic folk knew and practiced construction using cut stones more than two thousand years ago. The writer of these lines himself discovered well-preserved ruins of a Halgadom on the Hohenstein near Rothenkreuz in Bohemia and on the Schatzberg near Iglau, a prehistoric fortification constructed from squared stones. Both of these stone structures indicate an age of at least two thousand years. The Viennese archeologist Dr. Hans Hauer, who unfortunately died before his time, also discovered a church of Wuotan in Lower Austria, which he described to me in a conversation in the following way: "It is a well-preserved rectangular structure still in use, free standing on all sides with a low entry door on each of the four sides and a large window over each of these. The doors are faced precisely toward the four cardinal points, but so low that the person entering was forced to bow down to the holy object inside upon entering. The interior space is completely empty." The location of this very important structure was not indicated by my friend, who has since passed away, since he was planning further investigations and publications about it, I understandably refrained from making further inquiries. Noteworthy is, however, the fact that it is a rectangular building since Wuotan's churches (also the one at Hohenstein which is a domed structure with two towers positioned along its axis) are usually round structures, or better said — still are today. For without doubt all circular chapels, which are called Karner [charnel houses] today, and which earlier served as baptismal churches [baptisteries], are Christianized Wutotan-churches, which according to the directive of Pope Gregory — because they were well-built — were not torn down but rather were re-consecrated to the Christian God after the idolatrous images — called by Gregory, as Tacitus had also called them, *simulacrae* — to wit, the symbolic holy tokens of the Wuotan cult — had been removed and presumably destroyed. Lower Austria, Moravia, Bohemia, Stiermark, Bavaria, etc., all have numerous examples of these that are preserved and are still in service today. And strangely, most of these exhibit sculpted works, which, despite all sorts of contrived interpretations, cannot be easily understood within the context of Christian symbolism, and so therefore refuge is taken in a makeshift interpretation whereby it is said that these were comic images made at the whim of the architects and craftsmen on a lark. This requires no serious rejoinder. But when these are compared to often highly artistic bronze works and other sculpted objects from prehistoric grave-finds, works that experts "venture" to ascribe to our Aryo-Germanic ancestors, and think that these finds prove the innovation in form, skill in execution and technical craftsmanship with which sculptors among our ancestors were already very familiar, there is really no reason to deny these artistic talents to their descendants who lived before, during and after the time of the Roman invasion in Germania, all he less so since all these puzzling works of art can be interpreted very simply and easily with reference to the hieroglyphics of Armanism. And much more! Also, the law of *Kala* is clearly expressed in these images, each of which contains three different meanings that have already been alluded to in some detail above with regard to the legend of the Kahlenberg near Vienna. But this *Kala* goes on throughout the Middle Ages and enjoys its artistic zenith in the so-called Gothic period such that every Gothic structure, but especially every Gothic cathedral, from its foundation stone all the way up to its capital stones or up to its turret-rose, speaks in a clear language which is today unfortunately no longer understood— that is, until it was rediscovered by me. When, in new Gothic church buildings, as for example the Votive Church in Vienna, the unity of the tracery is praised in preference over medieval structures, this is actually usually a misunderstanding, because the old master intentionally endowed each window, or whatever, with a different form of tracery, for each shows in its special tracery, a concealed Armanic body of knowledge composed in *Kala* such that the whole proud structure indicates a hidden revelation of Armanic *Wihinei* that had been concealed through *Kala*, and all of which was absorbed by the builders' lodge into the High Hidden Institution to be secreted away and transmitted for future centuries in their "poems" fashioned out of stone and brick to express in fixed stone an inner conviction through such memorial structures for future generations awaiting that time when the blindfold of hypnotic suggestion will fall away from our senses.

After all national feeling and thinking had sunk into a deep sleep during the third, even more bloody, era of oppression under Karl the Great Saxon-slayer — something we will come back to later — and the Gothic began to disappear, the remains of the Armanen gathered together out of the building lodges of the practical masons and stone-cutters and formed "the lodges of the free or liberated masons," and in so doing withdrew completely from practical masonry and only preserved all their traditional doctrines, customs, symbols and other forms of secret knowledge in their strictly exclusive circles dedicated to "speculative masonry." In 1717 the four remaining lodges were unified in London as the first Freemasonic Lodge, the forms of which were also accepted by the German secret brotherhoods of "free masons," and following the example of the English from then on called their builders' lodges [Bauhütten] "lodges" [Logen]. But today the spirit of Armanism has been completely erased from Freemasonry — from the English as well as from the German — it has not only become entirely international, but rather, what appears even more suspicious, to have completely sunk down into being a satrapy of the *Alliance Israélite*. Freemasonry obviously still plays with the ancient traditional teachings, customs, symbols along with the *Kala*, degrees and secret signs all without really knowing what they all mean, since for their present-day brothers they are soul-less shells and insoluble riddles, that cannot be reconciled with the orientalism with which they try to revive these symbols, such that the supposed secret of Freemasonry consists of the fact that it no longer contains a secret in the sense of Armanism, while its present-day secret— which is rather transparent — is concealed behind the meaningful phrase *Alliance Israélite*. *Actum ut supra*!(j) But we can thank ancient Freemasonry (up to the middle of the 19th century) for the true preservation of that secret science that was taken into the High Secret Institution, where it likely formed a more or less unintelligible doctrinal structure, that nevertheless was not entirely lost, but now will once more come alive— but only if the key is found. The ancient builders' lodges likewise deserve thanks for their perseverance in the face of death in holding watch over the secret knowledge that they transmitted continuously in their works throughout times that seemed to be standing on the edge of the age of materialism that, it is hoped, held out an imminent promise of clarifying the world through a distant flaming twilight of the idols for the sake of a brighter, more light-filled ascent of the spirit. The person desiring knowledge will, however, fruitlessly seek a confirmation of what has been said here in the voluminous literature on art, art-history, types of style, etc., and so it brings me the most profound joy to be able to make reference to the groundbreaking work of the royal senior primary school teacher for architectural science, Herr B. Hanftmann in Magdeburg[37] who is also to be counted among those who see and know, and who, in his book, brought previously unknown things in the area of the architectural symbolism into view in both words and images. Likewise, Herr Director Friedrich Fischbach in Wiesbaden is one of the first out of many who has courageously come forward to explain such symbols, although too few of them have been known and honored, and whose books and writings have appeared which are herewith highly recommended. Just as with the "builders' lodges" with their many-formed branches, so too have heraldic fellowships [heralds] preserved Armanic secret knowledge in their manifold ramifications right up to the present day, and once more in another arrangement of *Kala*. They preserved the entire pictographic script (hieroglyphics) of the Armanen unbroken and almost intact up to the present day and their direct heirs, the modern heralds, cultivate — in the coats-of-arms — this pictographic script, certainly without knowing its true meaning, which only I have been successful in interpreting and reading. But they have also remained loyal to their true Armanic wisdom as well, defying many dangers and likewise, expressed in *Kala* and deeply hidden, they concealed their secret knowledge in encoded images awaiting more light-filled times, which can only now be decoded and made use of. To this group, however, also belonged the first three great chivalric orders of knights: the Teutonic Knights, the Knights of St. John (Malta) and the Templars, and those who read the history of the Templar trials as men of knowledge (Armanen), for them the puzzles cease to be puzzles, for they see at first glance that the knights of the order were *Kalanders*.

Here is the origin of the so-called Maltese-cross, the configuration of which constitutes two oppositional swastikas (*Hakenkreuze*). This extremely ancient Wuotanistic holy-sign (Fyrfos, Thor's Hammer) concealed (*verkalt*) here as a Christian cross is one that the brothers of the order wore on their chests, and that even today forms the basic type of almost all modern decorations of honor. And here the opportunity is also provided for the origin of the transition to the Christian cross and the crucifix to demonstrate how the cross was conquered in the sign of the cross, in a process — as shown in the example using the Maltese Cross — in which the *Kalandars* were active.

The simple straightforward cross + with four equilateral arms was the ancient Aryan sign of increase (plus) which the Romano-Christian evangelists contrasted with the Latin cross with a lengthened lower arm †.|38| A cross within a circle ⊖ was the sign of the court (*Feme*-Cross), which in the beginning was opposed to the Roman efforts, but which soon appears to have been taken over by the Church, to be replaced by the similar shaped *Hakenkreuz* ✛ that the priests opposed, calling it the "heathen cross." This struggle then soon generated those specialized cross-forms in which the *Hakenkreuz* is represented in *Kala*-forms.

It was very understandable that the earliest Christians, at the time when the so-called cross was still a despised tool of execution and therefore an offensive symbol, disdained depictions of the crucifixion of Jesus, and through the centuries stubbornly refused to depict the crucifixion scene, which appeared to them as something shameful, or to allow the image to appear before them. We also saw in the *Heliand*, as well as with Otfried in his Gospel-epic, how difficult it was for the authors of these two works to portray the death of Jesus and the events which led to, and accompanied, it in an appropriate manner in order not to damage the exalted divine image for impartial minds, whom they wanted to target with their message. The same difficulties were had, however, centuries earlier by the messengers of the Gospel among those peoples who were won over to Christianity earlier than the Germanic folk. The oldest depictions of Jesus are therefore that of the "Good Shepherd" or of the Lamb [*agnus Dei*], and it was not until the fourth century when these images were connected to the Cross, where the Lamb was at the foot and Jesus appeared as a bust, and shown at the terminals of the Cross or at its cross-point. Only in the fifth century does Jesus appear to be affixed to the cross with four nails. But still not dying, but rather with his head held high, portrayed more in a symbolic manner rather than a natural one. Between the years 424-460 a depiction of the crucifixion appeared on the wooden doors of St. Sabina's in Rome and there is supposed to be one of the same age as an ivory relief in the British Museum. Only in the sixth century do these depictions become realistic, showing the dying or dead Jesus, as, for example, the image in the Syrian manuscript of Rabulus in the Bibliotheca Laurentiana in Florence and the image of the crucifixion of Acheria of the Pallium Portificum in Egypt. But the dying Jesus was not depicted everywhere, since for a long time the Germanic peoples could not accustom themselves to a "dying god" in such a realistic setting, because even if "Wuotan sacrificed himself" this was seen as a mystical process free from outside human coercion. Thus, we see in the eleventh century and later, e.g. on the beautiful crucifix of the collegiate church at Innichen in the South Tyrol, the crowned Jesus with his head uplifted fixed to the cross by four nails (ones with three nails only occur after the twelfth century) below a giant head. And this too is once more *Kala*, as the "talking head" (Mime's head, the talking head of the Templars: "Baphomet" |*baf* = "pant; resound, speak loudly"; *om* = "the holy name (*omen, amen*) of God; *met* = "portion, measure," that is to say: "Each has a share of the main knowledge of the resounding name of God"| speaks to everyone who wants to hear it, i.e. who understands its language, i.e. who is a man of knowledge. There were many such "talking heads" most usually as containers of relics, as, for example, in the famous Guelph Treasure,(k) (two of which are extant) and which takes on the legend, e.g. that of the brother of Baco, that these heads were gifted with the ability to speak, which is once more an example of *Kala*. Only after a long struggle did the realistic crucifixion scene emerge victorious over the symbolic version and over the course of centuries the Germans became accustomed to the image of God being killed by humans, as they became accustomed to many other things as well.

As the influence of the *Kalanders* became weaker and weaker, the foundations which these had given to the Roman church in Germany increasingly decayed and faded and so we also soon came to see the "Black Mother of God" being displaced and overcome by the "Sorrowful Mother of God," and in only a few places of pilgrimage tenaciously held onto their ancient traditional images and customs. Completely in the same spirit, the ancient connection to triplicy emerged linked to other newly arising or otherwise renewed ancient triads of saints: "Arising, becoming, transforming" — obscured or forgotten, so that with the triad: Margaret, Catherine, Barbara; Fides, Spe, Charitas and others, the third one no longer appeared as being dark (as a Moor), but rather as light as the others are. So too do numerous new saints emerge who in no way have any connection with *Kala*. Roman ecclesiastical practice remained the victor in every regard and set about violently destroying the last remnants of shrinking Armanendom.

In an organic collaboration the three great Armanen-groups of the Skalds, the builders' lodge with the heraldic fellowships and the Femanen under the leadership of the *Kalanders*, not only prepared and guided the transition and norms from Wuotanism to Christianity, but rather along-side of many other successes they also accomplished the under-appreciated great deed of having wrested from the ascetically oriented, life-denying and therefore misogynistic Church the service of Our Lady, or the Cult of Mary, in the eleventh century and with it Armanic divinization of woman and thereby also obtained Christian recognition and sanctification for the free civil position of women. From this perspective, the development of the Christian Cult of the Lady in those times is especially significant, so therefore the most important information should be provided here in an abbreviated overview. From the fourth to the fifth century the question of the virginity of Mary was the focus of ecclesiastical controversy which was addressed in the fifth century with the main question of whether she was more precisely defined as the Mother of Christ or the Mother of God, which was resolved by ecclesiastical sanction in favor of the latter designation. In the sixth century, the festival of Maria Candlemas [Maria *Lichtmess*] was instituted, motivated by Armanic reasons, then the festival of the Annunciation of Mary [Iduna, swallows] and the Visitation of Mary [Processions Dispensing the Blessings of Frouwa]. In the eighth century, the Ascension of Mary (Freya with the cat-drawn chariot). In the eleventh century, the Saturday of every week was ecclesiastically dedicated to "Our Merciful Lady" (as it had been holy to Frouwa since ancient times) so that in 1095 Pope Urban II instituted a Saturday Officium in all monasteries. Thus the Lady Cult experienced a steady increase in its mystical component which should have led to the full recognition of the feminine priesthood in the Church just as it had been found in Wuotanism, but the Church endeavored to prevent this, by trying to reinstitute realistic aspects displacing mystical components by means of the addition of new Mary-festivals. A series of Mary-days were instituted which strongly emphasized human-feminine characteristics [The Wedding of Mary, etc.] into which older Mary-festivals [Candlemas as a Purification of Mary, etc.] were coordinated. By these means the hoped-for recognition on the part of the Church of a feminine priesthood broke down right at the beginning of the process, and could never rise above the quasi-priesthood of nunnery. But not satisfied with that, the Church wanted to get rid of this question for all time into the future as well and therefore immediately proceeded, according to its negative attitude, to go on the offensive, which it well-knew how to cloak in that it conducted the attack behind the pretense of the persecution of heretics as the main blow against the occult-oriented, mediumistic character of Germanic women, through which Papal Rome had assumed a hate toward Aryo-German-ness from the Rome of the Caesars, as an inheritance from them— and unleashed something like a scorching simoom against Germania, and thereby all efforts to obtain the priestly office for Germanic women, as well as any further development of the cult of the feminine in a mystically divine direction, was brought to an end with terror and horror. When the witchcraft persecutions are seen from the perspective of persecutions of heretics this most gruesome epoch of cultural developments in human history appears in an especially harsh and terrible light, for it all too clearly shows that the life-denying and therefore misogynistic Church was willing to go to such devilish means to defend itself against the threat of a feminine priesthood. World history cannot offer any other similar example of this sort.(n)[38] As a result of the consequences imposed by the Roman Church they did not, however, leave off with this one step, but in this context there unfolded the whole struggle over the ordination of priests in Catholicism, and the victory of the

Celibates in the eleventh century was a natural result of all of these efforts whose final aim was to be a fixed hierarchy and complete hegemony of Papal Rome over all of humanity.

With the Bull *Summis Desiderantes* of the 4th of December 1494 and the *Malleus Malificarum* of 1489 by Krämer and Sprenger(o) the main strikes on the part of the Church against Wuotanism or the counter-beliefs ("superstitions:") were made, and once these had been brought into effect these old beliefs began to lose all their conscious independence and were utterly brutalized.

That "witchcraft" [G. *Hexentum*] was originally nothing other than the secretly cultivated feminine priesthood of the holy female advisors [G. *Heilsrätinnen*], and the "witch-dances" only meant the secretly cultivated ancient Wuotanic festivals of nature, all needs no further proof.[40] But just how little of the truth was known at the time of the composition of the *Witches' Hammer* (1489), or perhaps also how they did not want to admit the truth, is proven in that in the preface to the *Witches' Hammer* the impression is given that they were confronting a completely new phenomenon. And documentary evidence certainly exists which indicates that already in the tenth century the order of witchcraft [*Hexenorden*] had been established according to the same principles as those found at the end of the fifteenth century, it was just at that time there were none of the ugly and tasteless suspicions which are later represented in the witch-trials with such sensational and barbaric nonsense.

Bishop Burkhart II of Worms, who died in 1024, already mentioned the services to the Devil during gatherings of women, which were certainly nothing other than that which was characterized as "witch-dances" in those documents connected to the witch-trials. Such a gathering, which he called a *consortium*, admitted women as members, who were all — in his opinion — deceived by the Devil [*a diabolo deceptae*] although they had to come to the gathering by his command [*ex praecepto*]. Of special importance is that according to his report every member of such a gathering was called "*Holda*" in popular speech [*vulgaris stultita*]. Holda or Hulda is, however, one of the names of the mother of the gods and queen of heaven, Frouwa, who — herself a sorceress — is the wife of the highest connoisseur of sorcery: Wuotan. In popular speech therefore, these witches were known as Holdas [G. *Holden*], therefore they had not yet come to be considered "*Unholden*" ("fiends"), as they would be thought of a half a millennium later. It is no less noteworthy that Bishop Burkhart further reports about how these *Holden* (witches) ride on animals; that is in no case on brooms and pitchforks as was later believed. That he has the women summoned by a number of devils points to his hatred against Wuotanism, whose divine figures were from the beginning always suspected of being devils by the Roman clerics, all of which is conceivable from an ecclesiastical viewpoint. Otherwise Bishop Burkhart is completely silent about what actually took place in these gatherings of "*Holden*," which obviously indicates that already at Burkhart's time witchcraft was more a matter of custom than any sort of teaching. These gatherings were just secret meetings of the Wuotanists which originally were under the leadership of secret Armanendom, the *Kalands*, who later — as we showed above in connection with Wiegand von Theben, the pastor of Kahlenberg from the year 1337 — became ever rarer, finally only to be linked to individual personalities who naturally, due to deficiencies in schooling were steadily educated in increasingly defective ways so that they eventually completely died out. Through this means the teaching was lost to the masses, but **the outer customs were retained**, but now deteriorated from the conscious and virtuous direction into vulgar orgy-like revels and debauchery. The previous divine sexual service, the final goal of which was to breed a noble race in a conscious manner only degenerated at this time to a kind of phallus-worship similar to that of the Dionysians and Floralians(m) of the kind that was never known in the pre-Christian Wuotanistic age, and with the passage of time sank down below this level into further degradation to a low level of swampiness. Already at the time of Emperor Otto I the nobility began to withdraw from those Wuotanistic festivals, and examples of their participation such as that of Duke Otto the Merry [1301-1339] from the year 1337 are exceptions, which can be recognized as such an exception in that the people withdrew when they found out the duke was to participate. The same phenomenon was seen later in the Rococo and *Zopf*-style times, during which the so-called better classes of people began to withdraw from the old folk-festivals which quickly caused these to become cruder and to decay, while for those who thought they belonged to better circles, the time of pastoral plays, of Italian operas and French salons had begun. The effect was the same. Once the folk-festivals had fallen out of fashion, they remained uniquely consigned to the people of the country-side, who still even today celebrate the summer solstice festival, the water-fowl festival and other similar ones that have long since been forgotten in the cities. All the same, the nobility had kept its distance from the Wuotan-mysteries and the subsequent witch-cult for about a millennium, and these were left to the peasant population, but there in a different way — it had become its own fashion. But by the time such an ancient folk-custom finally dies out, it will have long since lost its meaning; the spirit has been erased from it, and that which continues to exist as an apparent form of life, as a custom, is only an empty shell, a corpse without a soul. This was the case in the tenth century with the gatherings of the Holden, which had sunk down to a "cult without teaching," to the level of meaningless custom, just as happened at the end of the eighteenth century with the folk-festivals, which had already long since lost their mystical-religious meaning in the sense of Wuotanism. The class of peasants, who had long since been rendered unfree, which through planned repression, through intentional and systematic de-education, suppressed to the lowest level of cultural ignorance, made to be uncouth and almost animalistic, now formed almost the only link to the declining Wuotan-mysteries, because the few Armanen in the cities and in the castles had lost all sympathy with the people in the country-side, and also with the traditions of the "common folk on the heath," who had been formed from those Wuotanists who had been driven out or fled, were likewise rendered so depleted in spirit and made so crude in such a way that precluded them from being able to influence the customs of the peasants in any vital or enlightening way. And so, the last echoes of the Wuotan-mysteries sank down ever deeper such that by the time period of the witchcraft trials, or approximately a the beginning of the seventeenth century, they had disappeared completely.

The other Wuotanistic festivals of nature were preserved for a longer time, many right up to the present day, and once more acquired in the most recent times more space and meaning, but certainly only as popular festivals, for in the Wuotanist sense they can never again be renewed any more than a corpse can be made to breathe again, but they will build a bridge for a return to nature, and with that a new development of a higher honoring of nature which will be called upon to close the gap which has been established between faith and knowledge, and which today seems so irreconcilable.

If we examine the teachings presented by Jesus of Nazareth in more detail, however, we find that they too were founded upon the same esotericism or secret doctrine that the *Wihinei* of Armanism recognized; they were just the one and true religion that rested **"upon the awareness and recognition of a spiritual existence upon which the world depends, intimately and insolubly connected to the All."** But Jesus recognized all too well that his own people, his contemporaries and those of his kind would not be able to comprehend his teaching; therefore, he too communicated the esoteric secret doctrine only to his most trusted followers — the twelve Apostles — while he tried to explain the exoteric lore to the other seventy-two disciples or pupils in his incomparable parables.

It is Paul who was the creator of that system of religion that we today call Christianity, as he placed the person of Jesus at the center of attention, Jesus as the exemplary representative of the life of a god-man demonstrating the relation between God and humanity, and taught that he was the personification of the divine revelation to humanity and at the same time that he was conceived of logically as the second personality, of the Trinity, as the Son of God. Thusfar Christianity would have remained in harmony with the one, eternal religion of the *Wihinei* of Armanism, with the god-man — that is, the highest developed individual egos of the species *homo sapiens* — which existed and still do exist in all time periods. It is they who cause progress, and in an inspired state lead the masses to their own inspiration and toward higher aims. Since such god-men, who in their time had attained the highest level of knowledge, but also at the same time that height which rose above the level of humanity, thus they were — and are still today — in possession of that extraordinary divine power-modality which still slumbers within less developed humans and who are anxiously awaiting further development. They had already risen up in their previous earthly lives — from their present reincarnation —to that height which brought them close to divinity so that functioning in the next highest spiritual level they are freed from a renewed incarnation in an earthly life in a human body and due to a completely extraordinary duty they voluntarily, according to their own free choice, cause themselves to be reborn into a folk- or family-circle outside the normal line of descent in order to accomplish some great developmental act. But since they belong to the Earth and to its spiritual realm — which is the Earth-spirit itself — they are therefore bound to this realm until it passes away, i.e. until all ego-consciousnesses have been lifted up and been unified with the Earth-spirit [with the god of the Earth], in order to return back in this unified state to the sun-god, from which they emanated in the past. But since Paul insisted upon the recognition for Jesus of Nazareth as the *unique* god-man — excluding all others of the past or future — he thereby removed himself from the one true religion and created a religious system— Christianity.

By means of this introduction of an intercessor between God and humanity, the further distancing of Christianity as a religious system from the one true religion [*Wihinei*, Armanism] was completed; for now God was thought of as being outside the human heart — "up there in heaven" — and the genuine inwardness of God atrophied at the root. Still more! — Paul further fabricated the Old Testament doctrinal structure on the foundation of the Messianic concept in that he combined the essence of the New Testament within the concept of the perfect religion of salvation and reconciliation. The natural result was that man had to forget and repress all his innate intuition, and feelings of his own moral impotence and helplessness were repressed down to the deepest levels, whereby there developed a stifling despair with false feelings of moral guilt together with such an invalid penitent confessional attitude of limitless sinfulness and a faint-hearted longing to confess. Under this pressure, the law of reincarnation, which was recognized by Jesus himself, disappeared entirely, the dogmas concerning temporal and eternal punishments — the flames of Hell — as well as eternal reward — the heaven of the blessed and saints — confused and obscured the recognition of reincarnation more and more, until it finally — even as a secret Christian doctrine — completely disappeared. Through the dogma of the forgiveness of sins, by means of the prescribed "priest in the stead of God," not only was the law of Garma obscured and forgotten, but rather also the feeling of self-responsibility was clouded, such that the public and private morality of the folk was considerably damaged.

Other dogmas and customs of this religious system, which is really only to be considered as a church of priests, had similar damaging and most ruinous effects on the folk through its almost millennium and a half of hypnotic suggestion working from the outside, and if the one true religion — Armanism — had not been permanently planted in the heart of every member of the Aryo-Germanic folk, so that he is influenced unconsciously to return to its feelings, thoughts and deeds over and over again, then our glorious German folk

[*Deutschvolk*] would have long since gone its way along the path to Orcus, toward destruction, as did Rome and Byzantium in spite of the supposed culture-promoting effects of Christianity.

The pure exalted Armanen-lore, which Jesus of Nazareth promulgated in a new way, was obscured by Paul when he created his religion-system — Christianity. As its protector and promoter — the priest-church — made it all completely incomprehensible and unbelievable; such that it was and remains something implemented by violence using every method of overt coercion to support and protect the faith throughout time, a faith which is today little more than a means of exercising power on a partisan basis in order to serve certain social and class interests for which it serves as a final undermining bulwark. This priest-church, which had, and still has, every serious intention of de-nationalizing us Aryo-Germanic folk and among these most especially us Germans, placed us into a hypnotic trance condition which we are just now beginning to shake off — although we are in a weakened state and very sick but not yet beyond healing. Now there is already a second danger from another hypnotic suggestion approaching from the outside, or better said already from within in our midst — **the yellow peril** — and this yellow peril is called **Buddhism**.(p)

As the Christian doctrine of humility found in every denomination within the priest-church degenerated into a doctrine of servitude, so too did the doctrine of **resignation** in Buddhism begin to threaten our future with **a true and authentic Asiatic slave-religion**.

Buddhism in all its shades is based on the one true religion, which Armanism also recognizes in strict connection with the original eternal and immutable "primeval laws of nature" [*Natur-Ur-Gesetze*], it therefore has the same roots as Wuotanism and Christianity, but it in no way takes a back seat to Christian theology in its confusing levels of sophistry. Its theosophy is also founded in Armanism in a genuine manner as regards its roots, but what strikes many as deceiving are its conclusions and practices with regard to life, as it departs significantly from Wuotanism at its exoteric level. While Wuotanism guides us toward spiritual and physical heroism, as shown above, the asceticism of Buddhism places the body under the authority of the spirit — in the macrocosm as well as the microcosm — Buddhism diffracts and disdains all things physical [although without God's will it could not even exist!] and cultivates only that which is purely spiritual — the abstract. Meanwhile, Wuotanism explains the individual ego-ness as an indivisible part of the all-encompassing singular individuality [*All-Ein-Ichheit*] (of the All-Ego) and subordinates and incorporates this, but without robbing the ego-self of its rights as an individuality or ego-self. Buddhism isolates each individual ego which only participates in the cultivation of the individual ego over time, in order to achieve as quickly as possible its entry into Nirvana, that state of the god-man, who is liberated from any further reincarnation in the world of humans. While Wuotanism recognizes the foundation of every individual ego in the context, and for the benefit, of the All-Ego as a matter of duty, but also as a virtue which rewards the individual ego, whereas Buddhism recognizes this duty only in the context of activity as good works, such as giving alms, patience, etc., but this only in order to acquire individual merit, but not something for the benefit of the All-Ego. The same is true for the high moral recognition of Garma in Armanism as well as in Wuotanism, which only knows causes and their effects giving rise to eternally generative effects induced by those causes which can be either evil or good and accordingly express their results without these results necessarily being applicable. In Buddhism this is shifted into the doctrine of Karma and the concept of obligation is transformed into one of sin. The law of causality is by then obscured, as it comes to mean: "For every evil deed or omission you will suffer." The concept of punishment is then connected to this and the bad consequences [*Folgeübel*] are vaguely indicated, preparing the way for the forgiveness of sin by means of atonement and penance, i.e. the transmutation of bad consequences [*Folgeübel*] into a milder or more limited degree, so that now it comes out: "You will have to bear the consequences of your actions or omissions — whether in the good or bad sense — yourself, without you being able to ameliorate or lessen them in any way," as Armanism and Wuotanism most definitely emphasizes. In the obscured weakening of the awareness of "Garma" into the doctrine of "Karma" the great difference between Armanism and Wuotanism on the one hand and Buddhism on the other is made clear such that the Aryo-German does not view Garma as an unavoidable fate, but rather as a self-created destiny, which serves to increase his power, while the Buddhist gives himself over, as he sees it, to this unavoidable fate, but then seeks to ameliorate the consequences of this by means of penances.

A comparison between German and Buddhist folk-tales which deal with this theme will, better than any deeply researched discussion, confirm what has been said here. Certainly, one should not compare the Buddhism that has been transplanted here to Europe to that found in Lhasa or Ceylon or China or Japan, for there, it has also already descended to a low-point as a priest-church. But that form of Buddhism offered to us Europeans as a sort of esotericism has also ceased to be a true esotericism, and is rather on its way to becoming a religion-system, that is already beginning to develop the most refined enclosures, landing quietly and secretly in the well-concealed harbors for a priest-church of the future.

Taking the results of the present study into account, it can be shown that the Aryo-Germanic folk, and therefore our own German nation, not only since ancient times, have been in possession of the one true religion, which they developed further and today deepen and continually expand with ever more profoundly investigated recognition of nature, in which we comprehend with a basic understanding the uniqueness of the dyadic-dy-unitarian duo-unity [*zweispältig-zweieinige Zwei-Einheit*] of the spirit-body of the All and therefore also the eternity of the conscious individual ego throughout all of its metamorphic phenomenal forms, as well as of the strictly ordered structure and development of Garma, despite all foreign suggestion inwardly in any case — even if often unconsciously — all preserved as an inner religion although outwardly appearing to convert to Christianity, the apparent form of which was only an outward thing and therefore entirely secondary.

For this balanced care regarding the psycho-physical aspect they do not only have their political independence (as Germans) to thank, but rather also their world-domination (as Aryo-Germanic folk: Germans, Englishmen, Dutch, Lowlanders, Danes, Swedes, Norwegians, etc.) out of which there will develop a "Pan-Germanic Germany" [*Pangermanisches Deutschland*] in the future, because this must be formed in order to oppose all of the counter-obstructions put up by the dark powers. In contrast these realms (Greece, Rome, Byzantium, etc.) disappeared without a trace, since they only paid homage to material aspects, and entirely denied the spiritual ones, so that after they experienced a short period of apparent flourishing before they each fell, while those peoples who cultivated the spiritual and neglected the physical (material) things actually saved their kind, but were completely enslaved by foreign peoples to be dominated and exploited.

We Aryo-Germanic folk can only be protected from such destinies by our innate religion — the Armanic *Wihinei!* — as it protected us in earlier times and therefore we do not have much to fear from foreign suggestions, since we are still strong enough to defend ourselves from such things. But protecting ourselves from new dangers on the horizon always remains a part of the law of providential intelligence.

Textual Notes by List

These are notes provided by List in the text of the book. They often consist of cross references to his other works, only a few of which have been translated at this juncture. Where translations exist, the English titles are given.

|1| The Greco-Roman geographers and historiographers (Julius Caesar, Tacitus, Ptolomy, *et al.*) erroneously recorded their names as Irmiones, Hermanes, Semnones and mistakenly called them, in complete misunderstanding of the situation, *tribes* of people rather than *classes* of people.

|2| Garmic = karmic.

|3| Enough for the wise.

|4| About this see the excellent book: *Das Professorentum der Stolz der Nation?* by privy councilor Prof. Max Seiling in the Verlag Mutze, Leipzig, 1905.

|5| See more about Garma, garmic chains and garmic laws as well as the interpretation of the name "German" in my work The Religion of the Aryo-Germanic Folk: Exoteric and Esoteric in the third volume of the Deutsches Wiedergeburt |German Rebirth| series. Published by Dr. Ernst Wachler, Verlag Adolf Bürdeke Zürich 1910.

|6| *Die Rita der Ario-Germanen*, third volume of the Guido-von-List-Bücherei.

|7| More details on this in the two volumes of the Guido-von-List-Bücherei No. 2 *Die Armanenschaft der Ario-Germanen* and No. 4 *Die Völkernamen Germaniens und deren Deutung*. The Greco-Roman authors erroneously designated these estates as tribes.

|8| *Rachakater*, from *raha* = G. *Rache* ("vengeance"); *kater* = fighting people, warriors — G. *Recke* ("hero") from *raha, rehe* = "vengeance," therefore "avenger." — Circulator, i.e. "those who 'ran on the journey,'" therefore emigrants, mercenaries |G. *Landesknechte*| servants obtained by the country, soldiers, paid troops; not knights |G. *Lanzknechte*| for they bore no lances, the chivalric weapon, but rather only spears and halbards.

|9| During the Crusades the Crusaders found to their great astonishment German-speaking tribes in Palestine and in the campaign of Emperor Charles V to Tunis the Berbers greeted the Germans as their relatives. In both of these cases the ancient remnants of old Aryo-Germanic colonies can be recognized. And similar examples could be cited in ancient Egypt, Persia and India.

|10| For more on this see Guido-von-List-Bücherei No. 4 *Die Völkernamen Germaniens und deren Deutung*.

|11| See more about this in my book *The Religion of the Aryo-Germanic Folk*.

|12| See more about this: Guido-von-List-Bücherei Nos. 2, 3 and 5 where the origin and meaning of crosses in connection with the *Armanenschaft* is exhaustively handled.

|13| In Sanskrit, likewise an Aryan sister language of the Aryan *ur*-language, *kal* means "time" and *Kaly* a cycle of time or era |*kal*| = time; *li* |*ly*| = "course," that is a course of time or section of time, an era. From this, for example, the Kali-Yuga = the religious era of the Buddhists; the black, actually dark, goddess of death, Kali, etc. In Finnish, according to age-old Aryo-Germanic traditions, the great mythic epic of the Finns is called the *Kalevala*, i.e. the death of time, the end. The folkloric epic of the Estonians is called, with the same meaning in the name, the Kalevi-poeg. Similarly, the holy bird of Indian mythology is called the Kaly-hamsa, which is related to the world-egg (cf. Leda and the Swan). Such corroborating examples could be expanded, but these should be sufficient.

|14| Brief illustration of the *Kaland* by Martin Blumberg. Chemnitz in Saxony 1721. Leuckfeld. Antiquarian. Gröning. — Keysler Antiqu. Sept. et Celtic p. 559 Beckmann's Anhalts Hist. VI.4.

|15| Guido von List. *Deutsch-Mythologische Landschaftsbilder* 1891 Lüstenöder, Berlin.

|16| More about the symbolism of this and its secret sign see: Guido-von-List-Bücherei Nr. 5 *Die Bilderschrift der Ario-Germanen*. Vienna: Guido-von-List-Gesellschaft, 1910.

|17| Compare Tacitus' *Germania* and others. But especially should be noted that a Catholic bishop gave the Arian Vandals the highest praise, and it is important to remind our contemporaries as often as possible of this. It was the Bishop of Marsilia, present-day Marseille, Sabianus, a contemporary of the Vandals, who wrote in his letters about the government of God: "There is no virtue in which we Romans are superior to the Vandals. We abhor them as heretics (because they were Arians), and yet they are our superiors when it comes to their fear of God. God has placed them, the Vandals, over us in order to chastise the unchaste peoples through their purity of custom. — — — "Wherever the Goths rule no one is unchaste except the Romans, where the Vandals rule, even the Romans become chaste."

|18| Among these are counted Till Eulenspiegel, the Pastor Amis and many another jester and jolly councilors as well as other so-called humorists of the Middle Ages, which can only be discovered by means of *Kala* which we will have the opportunity to return to later. For our present purposes, we will just pick out one example.

|19| Apostle of the English.

|20| See the author's *The Religion of the Aryo-Germanic Folk*.

|21| These names too are *Kala*: Gastibor: *gast* |*kast*| = enclosed; *ibor* |*ebor*, *ebor* = stork, boar (G. *Eber*), etc.| = birth, arising; therefore enclosed, hidden origin. — Melichari: *melich* = gradually |G. *mählich*| *ar* = sun; *ri* = growth; therefore, gradual growth of the sun. — Balthasahar *bal* = sun; *tha* = position, standing; *sahar* = burning, scorching [Sahara]; therefore "the solar position of burning, solar death."

|22| *men* can also be read as "moon." Then it would mean: coercive man, coercive month.

|23| With regard to the "six days" |G. *sechs Tage*| — *sex tag* — it should be recalled what I said in my earlier work about the *Religion of the Aryo-Germanic Folk* with reference to the "mysticism of numbers" concerning "sex" |sexuality|, which is here concealed in *kala* in the same way showing that those six days are based on "sex-days." The first six days of

the Twelve memorialize the generation of the world or creation of the All, the second six days of the Twelve are those of the creation of humanity. And the circumstance that the "Great New Year," that falls on the sixth day of the new year, that actually ushers in Fasching, only becomes meaningful in that just this sixth day stands at the head of the festival time as the sex-day.

The *Faschingskrapfen* [Fasching-pastry], the well-known sacred pastry is also connected to this. Its name is formed from the two *ur*-words, *kar* and *ap*: *kar* = "contained', *ap* = "turn, round [apple], movement [ape], life"; therefore "contained life," that will now come to fruition in the festival time.

Wherever we listen to our German mother-tongue, everywhere it speaks to us in the most meaningful images as the most genuine poetic language, more full of blossoms in this regard than the badly overestimated language of the Orient! — Germans, once and for all learn to understand your mother-tongue!

[24] In the *Rau*-nights, considered "oracle-nights," understandably games of chance and skill had great meaning, and of course the ancient Germanic game of dice and no less games of cards, board-games and bowling. Director Friedrich Fischbach (Wiesbaden) writes the following in his highly interesting essay in celebration of Gutenberg 1900 entitled *Ursprung der Buchstaben Gutenbergs* [Origin of the Letters of Gutenberg] (Mainzer Verlagsanstalt, 1900): "In my [Fischbach's] possession is an Alexandrian textile from the 3rd to 4th century, the pattern of which proves that our playing-card designs were holy symbols back then. A glance at the ornaments pertaining to the fire-cult proves connections between the altar-slab, the ivy-leaf and the cross that has been transformed into a trifolium (trefoil, clover-leaf). The Egyptian hieroglyph that indicates the tree of life (Yggdrasil) became a broadened lance, a pike; the playing-card symbol that we call the cross (*Treff*), is replaced on ancient German cards by an acorn, additionally, our square, cornerstone or carreau is replaced by a diamond-shape; just as the ivy-leaf

appears as a heart. The card of highest value is the Ace (Ase = god). The card with the number nine of the holy fire-platform (see below concerning the nine fire-mothers, etc.) has a special power connected to the idea of exchange. Wuotan and Freya are the king and queen; the farmer (*Bub*) is Thor, who not only protects farmers, but also often travels about dressed as a knave." From all this we can now also explain the origin of divination by means of "drawing playing cards."

The meritorious Germanist Dr. Franz Winterstein in Kassel published in *Westermanns Monatshefte* (1907, no. 12) a valuable illustrated essay: "Ein altgermanisches Spiel, Glocken- und Hammerspiel," out of which the following is excerpted:

Chimes and hammer-play belong to the perineal modes of entertainment during the long winter evenings and were happily practiced by young and old alike, especially around the time of the holy nights ... The main geographical area for this art form was and remains, by all indications, among the folk of Lower Saxony, from northwestern to southwestern Germany. [South-Germany as well as Vienna knew it quite well since olden times, which is just mentioned here as an aside to show that it was spread all over Germania!] In this regard [i.e. in regard to Wuotanism] the conspicuous position of "the white stallion," that is, the Stallion of Saxony is also noted, so the performance points to the "Slider" [Sleipnir] of Wuotan. The hammer is Donar's (Thor's) weapon, the [G. *Malmer* = Mjölnir] "Crusher," and the inn itself (in Saxon called a *Kaufhaus*, "purchase house") is he heavenly shelter "Walhall" in which Wuotan's guests, the Einherjar are served splendidly and which receives contributions from mortals. Following the rules of the game, the sacrifices to the father of the gods become even more clearly recognizable; here the game-markers (chips) are offered to his representative, the white horse. Whoever wants too much has to pay the reckoning in Walhall, all but the owner of the white horse. In the main, however, this game is a reference to a world-struggle originally occurring between Wuotan and Donar, a battle of words relating to the fortress of the gods .... Instead of the word-contest between Wuotan and Donar arose (in the time of the *Kalanders*) the contest between hammer and bell, between the old and new faith, between Wuotanism and Christianity and the final unification of the two in the card: "hammer and bell." This gave the name "bell- and hammer-game" to the play, which had previously probably had the name "horse and hammer game" or simply the "hammer game."

[25] The Ash [*Ask* = "arising"] as the fire-drill is the "fire-father." The nine fire-mothers [nine mothers of Heimdall] are: Alder [*yrla*] = "seeking life"; Oak = [*eok*] = "lawful excitement"; Scots pine [*for-ak*] = "fire-excitement"; Birch [*biark*] = "enclosed life"; Willow [*uid*] = "law"; Yew [*ybe, ube, auff*] = "knowledge, spirit"; Spruce [*fikte*] = "realm of generation"; Beech [*boke*] = "feminine bearer, offerer, connector, generator"; Fire [*tan-ne*] = "doing, bearing."

[26] Also called *Salvator*: *sal* = "salvation"; *vator* = "father, generator," therefore "generator of salvation," a byname of Wuotan, who is, as the Second Logos, likewise the Son of God.

[27] More details about this in Guido-von-List-Bücherei No. 2, *Von der Armanenschaft der Arier*.

[28] Sow = "generation of endurance"; *Rüssel* [= snout] = *ruozzen*: *ruo* = *rau* = right, Heil; *zen* = sun; therefore: "solar heil"

[29] The Church interprets the concept "carnival" in a deceptive way from *carne* = "flesh," *vale* = "farewell"; as the departure from the eating of meat due to the approach of the time of fasting.

[30] Möna from Mönak or mönask; *mön* = "moon, man, generator," *ak* or *ask* [3rd word-level] "reversed, destroyed, ash" therefore infertile. The same word also means Münnich, monk, without having to be derived from Latin *monachus*, since the Aryo-Germanic *ur*-language has the same *ur*-, bud-, root- and stem-words as Latin, and the older language has the same origin.

[31] Concerning numerical symbolism, see Deutsche Wiedergeburt No. 3: Guido List, *The Religion of the Aryo-Germanic Folk*.

[32] *The Religion of the Aryo-Germanic Folk* Guido von List, No 3 of the Deutsche Wiedergeburt.

[33] Guido-von-List-Bücherei No. 2 and 2A: *Von der Armanenschaft der Arier*.

[34] The exact same fate befell the Catholic monasteries at the time of the Reformation; they too were abolished, their property seized by the princes, and only a very small fragment was used for the new Protestant church. Indeed, it may be that the Reformation movement was greatly assisted by the enticement to confiscate church properties.

[35] Those who want to educate themselves about the details of the second era of the Christianization of Germania should buy the worthwhile little book *Der Tempel zu Rethra und seine Zeit* by P. Wigalois (Berlin-Mariendorf: Verlag G. Simons, 1907) since the depiction of these matters lies outside the limits of our work here, but to complete it in a significant way.

[36] I know very well that the Carolingian Walloons were not Ripuarians, but they were kings of the Ripuarian people and as such became the Ripuarian dynasty.

[37] Professor B. Hanftmann, architect B.d.A. "Hessische Holzbauten," contributions to the history of western German housing and wooden construction as an introduction to L Bichel's *Hessische Holzbauten* with 119 illustrations and a map. Marburg 1907. N. G. Elwert'sche Verlagsbuchhandlung 4 XVIII, 200 pages.

[38] More details in my work: *The Secret of the Runes*, *Die Armanenschaft der Arier* and in subsequent publications of the Guido-von-List-Society in Vienna. Likewise, in the context of the work in this series, *The Religion of the Aryo-Germanic Folk*, etc.

[39] Significant, and up to now much too little considered, is the situation that the witchcraft trials precisely differentiated between "witchcraft" [G. *Hexerei*] and "sorcery" [G. *Zauberei*], in that the former was punished by "living fire"

and the latter by "simple beheading." This clearly proves that the Church sought to destroy the witch as the most dangerous enemy of the ascetic doctrine as she was the mediumistically talented woman, preordained by divinity itself, since witch-masters only very rarely appear in the records of the witch-trials. Every witch was certainly in the view of the witch-master also a sorceress, while a sorceress did not always have to be a witch. That is enough reason to give us pause to think.

[40] The basis of witchcraft was the three degrees of the feminine priesthood of Wuotan, the Order of Holy Advisors, which was arranged according to the *Hag-Idisen* (Hexes, "Witches"), *Thruden* and *Walen* and were subject to the guidance of the *Albruna*. In early Germano-Christian times certainly gatherings and haling practices held by the Holy Advisors or Holden were also taken into the *Hohe Heimliche Acht* and secretly preserved there, whereby also the male leader of the gathering, who was an *Armane* and probably appeared in the guise of Wuotan, surrounded by a legendarily formed aura, all designed to scare the Christians. Therefore, due to this he was stamped as the Devil himself, for the Roman clerics called everything that was in any way connected to Wuotanism "devilish." As it became increasingly dangerous to participate in these gatherings, the people were finally no longer certain about spies and informants within their own camp, many appeared with masks or blacked out their faces in order to be unrecognizable, something that is often mentioned and verified in later accounts of witchcraft trials.

Editorial Notes

These are notes on the contents of the book by the editor and translator. These do not comment on the legitimacy or validity of the contents of the book, but merely clarify certain words or phrases and historical points of interest.

(a) The phrase *ver sacrum* is Latin for "sacred spring."

(b) the word *situlih* is Old High German meaning "according to custom," NHG *sittlich*.

(c) This is a translation of List's version of this letter, which is some details of word-choice does not necessarily always agree with more standard translations which are widely available. See Appendix B.

(d) List writes: that Golgatha "simply means "station of the gallows." the actual translation of the term is "place of the skull" from Hebrew *gulgōlet*, "skull."

(e) The Advent-Mass used the text from Issiah 45:8 from the Vulgate *Rorate coeli desuper et nubes pluant justum*: "Drop down dew, ye heavens, from above, and let the clouds rain the just." This was the basis for a German song entitled "Tauet, Himmel, dem Gerechten" written in 1774 by the Jesuit priest Michael Denis in Vienna.

(f) Here List writes the term "*Raunächte*," which would usually be written "*Rauhnächte*." This involves traditions first recorded in 1725, but which must go back to pagan times. The *Rauhnächte* are usually observed in the twelve days between the winter solstice and the sixth of January, or alternatively between St. Thomas (December 21 and New Year. This is the time period, according to tradition, when the souls of the dead, along with the "Devil," cause all sorts of mischief among the living. In order to protect themselves, people used incense (*Rauch*, "smoke") to cleanse their homes of evil influences. An alternate explanation of the name derives it from the word *rauh*, "rough," with reference to the rough character of the beastly creatures who run around keeping people awake at night. In the text List rejects both of these explanations in favor of an esoteric analysis of the word.

(g) Epiphania = Epiphany which is also known as Theophany in the East. It is considered the feast day that celebrates the revelation (theophany) of God incarnated in Jesus. In the West, this also is the time of commemoration of the visit of the Magi to Jesus and is called "Three Kings Day" or "Little Christmas."

(h) The names given in the printed version of List's text read *Ator, Eatar* and *Peratores*, which are considerably garbled forms of the names given in cap. I of a text published in 1764 by Antonio Sandini entitled *Historia Familiae Sacrae* as Ator, Sator and Paratoras or Pentoras.

(i) Current English words used here are: "Remember, O man, that you are dust, and unto dust you shall return."

(j) *actum ut supra*: "done as above," i.e. "see reference above."

(k) The Guelph Treasure was historically held at the cathedral at Brunswick (Braunschweig). The former Duke of Brunswick sold much of it to art dealers in 1929. Objects were widely dispersed in many museums. Hermann Göring acquired many objects from Dutch art dealers in 1935. Those pieces are now found in the Bode Museum in Berlin.

(l) *Summis desiderantes affectibus* (Latin for "desiring with supreme ardor") was a papal bull regarding witchcraft issued by Pope Innocent VIII on 5 December 1484. On the Protestant side the *Malleus Maleficarum* was produced as a sort of "witch-hunters' manual." $$$

(m) History of the Church reports: "The Lupercalia and Florealia were celebrated with a shameless disregard of decency, and the most obscene plays were presented in the theaters. The excesses of sensuality were carried to such a length that the natural means of satisfying lust were no longer sufficient, and recourse was had to the most degrading and unnatural of vices. The civic virtues also disappeared, to be replaced by every species of crime, and disregard of life and suicide ceased to be matters of surprise."

(n) As was once explained to your editor by a mystical Liberal Catholic bishop, the reason why women cannot be priests is a *magical* one. The ritual of the Eucharist is an elemental magical operation in which the Holy Spirit (thought to be a feminine entity) *naturally* requires a masculine counter-pole in order to call upon it to be infused into the bread and wine to cause transubstantiation. Women cannot be priests because this ritual is really the only major function of a priest and according to magical theory the ritual simply would not work with two feminine electro-magnetic poles. Female priesthood may have been a political topic, and this may just be a modern esoteric excuse, but it would account for the centuries of absolute stubbornness on the part of the Catholic hierarchy. Interestingly Reichsführer-SS Heinrich Himmler took up List's theory that the women victims of the widespread German witchcraft persecutions were actually remnants of the old Germanic female priesthood, one of whose main functions was the insurance of pure Germanic "bloodlines." (See my book *The Occult in National Socialism* Inner Traditions, 2022.)

(o) The *Malleus Maleficarum* has been translated into several languages from its original Latin. Montague Summers did one in 1929, but more recently an academic treatment has been produced: *The Hammer of Witches: A Complete Translation of the Malleus Maleficarum*, trans. by Christopher S. Mackay (Cambridge: Cambridge University Press, 2009)

(p) Among German Theosophists, e.g. Rudolf Steiner, there developed a strong anti-oriental stream. List certainly belonged to this camp, without agreeing with them on many other things.

(q) Many practicing Buddhists and Buddhistic scholars might find fault with List's apparent misunderstanding of Buddhism. According to Buddhist teaching the things mentioned are not inferior or superior, but rather neither are thought to *exist* at all, and are thought to be illusions.

Glossary

Guido von List used many special words in German, innovated some other terms, with a nod to Nietzsche, and borrowed others from various languages, especially Sanskrit. Many of these I have left untranslated, as they were not really part of standard German usage at the time in which List was writing. This glossary is therefore essential to the understanding of the contents of the book in general, and forms a useful resource for the understanding of Listian terminology in other contexts. See also the Glossary of Key Listian Terms by Lenthe (2018, pp. 253-271)

Armane pl. *Armanen*: A member of the social structure responsible for intellectual, spiritual, legal and artistic endeavors. Equivalent of the Brahmanic caste in India and the First Function in the system of Georges Dumézil.

Armanenschaft: The institutional form into which the Armanen organized themselves. It also alludes to the inner continuing set of ideas inherited from generation to generation among the reincarnated members of the ancient Armanen.

Aryo-Germanic: Relating to the people who originally came down from the polar regions, some of whom went to Asia (becoming the Aryo-Indians and Iranians, and some of whom went to Europe becoming the Aryo-Germans. The concept usually described as "Indo-European" in the English-speaking world is commonly referred to as "Indo-Germanisch" in the German-speaking realm.

Feme: Also spelled *Vehme*, was a medieval tribunal system especially active in Westphalia. They held secret courts (G. *heimliche Gerichte*) and had permission from the Emperor for their activity which often involved vigilante executions. The *Feme* was suppressed in 1811 during Napoleonic occupation. In the Weimar period in Germany the *Feme* was "revived" as a mythic framework for the activities of the *Schwarze Reichswehr*.

Fremdsuggestion: Hypnotic suggestion imposed on a person or an entire culture from the outside.

Garma: A Listian innovation based on the Sanskrit *karma*, "action." In the mythology of List, it is tinged with connotations connected to the apocalyptic dog, Garmr mentioned three times in the *Poetic Eddic*. For List Garma = Karma, but for some reason he did not want to borrow this term directly.

Garmic: Adjective relating to Garma above.

Halgadom: A Listian term meaning "a place of holiness." These sites were isolated in the forests and constituted communities of priests of Wuotan dedicated to esoteric studies.

High Holy/Secret Tribunal/Institution: The formulaic phrases *Hohe Heilige Acht* or *Hohe Heimliche Acht* appear frequently in the writings of von List. *Hohe*, simply means "high," the middle term varies between *heilige*, "holy" and *heimliche*, "secret." The third term has caused problems for translators. It could mean an "institution" of some kind, or a legal tribunal. For von List, it clearly means a conscious group or school of Armanen who are charged with translating and transitioning eternal Armanic wisdom through the ages.

Kala: Ultimately derived from Sanskrit through Theosophical understanding, it is a concept of time, cyclical time and the permutation of all things through cyclical levels of meaning and reality. It is a tool of interpretation by which various levels of meaning are discovered though code-words and sounds. The concept lies at the root of List's form of esoteric runology.

Kalander: These were the ancient initiates who knew how to use and interpret the *kala*.

kalic: Adjective relating to *Kala*, see above.

Minne: Middle High German word, derived from the concept "memory," which indicated the spiritual form of *love*. This was the word for the concept of "courtly love" and is contrasted with the word for physical or sexual love, *liebe*.

priest-church: List deems the Catholic Church to have become an institution primarily meant to serve the interests of its priesthood and not the people.

religion-system or religious system: List differentiates the many artificial systems of religion created by people throughout history with this term in contrast to the one true primeval religion of humanity, which he designates with the term *Wihinei* or Armanendom.

Rita: List borrows this word directly from Sanskrit. Sanskrit *rita* or *ṛta* means "cosmic order." This is the correct functioning of the universe, and hence the "natural law" upon which all human laws are rightfully based.

Secret Doctrine: this term is used consistently to translate the original German *Geheimlehre*, which is the title of the German translation of H. P. Blavatsky's *The Secret Doctrine*, the most essential work of Theosophy.

Tracery: The Gothic stone geometrical symbols used for apparently decorative purposes.

Ur: This is used as an independent word by List, although it is normally only found as a prefix. As a prefix, *ur-* indicates the "original" or "primeval" state of the concept to which it is affixed, e.g. *Urzeit*, "ancient times," etc.

Wihinei: This is the ancient term, according to List, for what we commonly call "religion" today. It is really the secret teachings of science and art as practiced by the ancient *Armanen* and preserved by the *Kalander* after the coming of Christianity. In the early Middle Ages the *Kalander* wove the ancient Armanic *Wihinei* together with Christian imagery in order to preserve it and pass it on to the future, to be decoded later by latter-day *Armanen* such as List. In no other book does List make it clearer that *Wihinei* is an ahistorical, *universal* form of wisdom or "religion" shared by all peoples, with each national or folk-group (such as the Aryo-Germanic folk) possessing their own historical forms, such as Wuotanism represents.

Appendix A
The Master Vindicated?

A memorial grave (*Tumbagrab*) is situated on the south side of the Cathedral of St. Stephen in Vienna. "On a sarcophagus-like substructure rests an incomplete recumbent sandstone figure depicting a man in a tall cap. This is supposed to be the grave of Neidhart Fuchs. Upon the opening of this grave in the year 2000 the bones of two different men were found together, one who apparently lived between 1110 and 1260 and who died at the age of between 45 and 55, the other is ascribed to the 14th century and died between the ages of 35 and 45. In view of this evidence it is possible that these are the bones of the poet Neidhart and that of the "peasants' enemy" Neithart Fuchs.

Appendix B

CHAP. XXX. A copy of the letter which Pope Gregory sent to the Abbot Mellitus, then going into Britain. [601 A.D.]

The aforesaid envoys having departed, the blessed Father Gregory sent after them a letter worthy to be recorded, wherein he plainly shows how carefully he watched over the salvation of our country. The letter was as follows:

"To his most beloved son, the Abbot Mellitus; Gregory, the servant of the servants of God. We have been much concerned, since the departure of our people that are with you, because we have received no account of the success of your journey. Howbeit, when Almighty God has led, you to the most reverend Bishop Augustine, our brother, tell him what I have long been considering in my own mind concerning the matter of the English people; to wit, that the temples of the idols in that nation ought not to be destroyed; but let the idols that are in them be destroyed; let water be consecrated and sprinkled in the said temples, let altars be erected, and relics placed there. For if those temples are well built, it is requisite that they be converted from the worship of devils to the service of the true God; that the nation, seeing that their temples are not destroyed, may remove error from their hearts, and knowing and adoring the true God, may the more freely resort to the places to which they have been accustomed. And because they are used to slaughter many oxen in sacrifice to devils, some solemnity must be given them in exchange for this, as that on the day of the dedication, or the nativities of the holy martyrs, whose relics are there deposited, they should build themselves huts of the boughs of trees about those churches which have been turned to that use from being temples, and celebrate the solemnity with religious feasting, and no more offer animals to the Devil, but kill cattle and glorify God in their feast, and return thanks to the Giver of all things for their abundance; to the end that, whilst some outward gratifications are retained, they may the more easily consent to the inward joys. For there is no doubt that it is impossible to cut off everything at once from their rude natures; because he who endeavors to ascend to the highest place rises by degrees or steps, and not by leaps. Thus the Lord made Himself known to the people of Israel in Egypt; and yet He allowed them the use, in His own worship, of the sacrifices which they were wont to offer to the Devil, commanding them in His sacrifice to kill animals, to the end that, with changed hearts, they might lay aside one part of the sacrifice, whilst they retained another; and although the animals were the same as those which they were wont to offer, they should offer them to the true God, and not to idols; and thus they would no longer be the same sacrifices. This then, dearly beloved, it behoves you to communicate to our aforesaid brother, that he, being placed where he is at present, may consider how he is to order all things. God preserve you in safety, most beloved son.

"Given the 17th of June, in the nineteenth year of the reign of our most religious lord, Mauritius Tiberius Augustus, the eighteenth year after the consulship of our said lord, and the fourth indiction."

Bibliography

Flowers, Stephen Edred. *The Revival of the Runes*. Rochester: Inner Traditions, 2021.

———. *The Occult in National Socialism*. Rochester: Inner Traditions, 2022.

Goodrick-Clarke, Nicholas. *The Occult Roots of Nazism*. Wellingboro: Aquarian, 1985.

Lenthe, Eckehard. *Wotan's Awakening*. Trans. Annabel Lee, ed. Michael Moynihan. Waterbury Center: Dominion, 2018.

List, Guido von. *Deutsch-mythologische Landschaftsbilder*. Berlin: H. Lustenoder, 1891, 2 vols.

———. *Das Geheimnis der Runen* (= Guido-von-List Bücherei 1) Gross-Lichterfelde: P. Zillmann, 1908.

———. *Die Bilderschrift der Ario-Germanen*. (= Guido-von-List-Bücherei 5) Vienna: Guido-von-List-Gesellschaft, 1910.

———. *Die Ursprache der Ario-Germanen und ihre Mysteriensprache*. (= Guido-von-List-Bücherei 6) Vienna: Guido-von-List-Gesellschaft, 1914.

———. *The Secret of the Runes*. Translated by Stephen E. Flowers. Rochester: Destiny, 1988.

Murphy, G. Ronald. *The Saxon Savior*. Oxford: Oxford University Press, 1989.

———, trans. *The Heliand*. Oxford: Oxford University Press, 1992.

Russell, James C. *The Germanization of Early Medieval Christianity* Oxford: Oxford University Press, 1994.

Thorsson, Edred. *The Runic Magic of the Armanen*. [unpublished MS, 1975].

———. *Runelore: A Handbook of Esoteric Runology*. York Beach: Weiser, 1987.

———. *Green Rúna: The Runemaster's Notebook: Shorter Works of Edred Thorsson. Volume 1 (1978-1985)*. Bastrop: Lodestar, [original 1996].

www.ingramcontent.com/pod-product-compliance
Lightning Source LLC
Chambersburg PA
CBHW031405160426
43196CB00007B/906